Three Feet from Death

REFLECTIONS ON AN AMAZING RESCUE

UNIVERSITY
of MARY PRESS

First published in 2024

Published in the United States of America
by University of Mary Press
7500 University Drive
Bismarck, ND 58504
www.umary.edu

ISBN: 978-1-7348826-7-4

Printed in Canada

Written in gratitude to our loving and merciful God who spared me from death on the day of my accident, to Our Lord and Savior Jesus Christ who bore the Cross for my salvation, to the multitude of heavenly intercessors who tugged the tassel of Jesus' cloak on my behalf at that moment, and the host of human intercessors whose prayers bore me up throughout the recovery process, the multitude of talented professionals who assisted me on the road to healing, the caring volunteers who walked with me in bearing this particular cross, the farmer-angel who first appeared on the scene and called the rescue team, and the gentleman whose truck wheels engaged my vehicle. This experience occasioned my re-awakening to the most important realities in life, seeking to live each day in readiness for our final moment on earth and entry into the next life.

In loving memory of my beloved parents now laid to rest where my body will one day join theirs, brother priests, family and friends who have gone on to prepare the way before me, the many unnamed saints of the parish communities I have served over the past half century, all those whose funeral rites I have been privileged to provide, and all who must be saying,
"He will be with us soon enough."

Table of Contents

1 Miracle and Marvel

"Oh my gosh! You survived that? You are a miracle!" This was the typical wide-eyed reaction of the many to whom I showed the picture you see on the front cover of this work. What you see there is the remains of my 2004 Oldsmobile Alero awaiting removal from the scene of the accident in which I was marvelously spared from death on September 14, 2021.

In the pages to follow, I will take you through the events of that day, my treatment and recovery process, and what I am learning about life and about God's grace following what I consider a serious wakeup call. In so doing, I hope every reader will reap some benefit for their own life journey, be it comforting, affirming, challenging, or some blend of all three.

The reflections I offer, based on my experience of the accident and recovery process, are based on Sacred Scripture and teachings of the Catholic Church, as you would expect from a Catholic priest such as myself. I will include several references to the Catechism of the Catholic Church and other relevant theological sources.

Christians of every tradition should identify well with the truths of Scripture presented here and can hopefully appreciate my references to our teachings and devotional practices while comparing them to your own spirituality. Readers unfamiliar with any of these realities should still benefit from your reflection on experiences like those I describe in the following chapters.

Let me briefly explain what you see in the picture before we proceed. The engine compartment of the Alero was crushed under the rear wheels of a semi-truck trailer coming from my left on a gravel road as I was travelling on the paved highway. Once I realized the truck was not going to stop at the intersection as it should, I slammed on the brakes in hopes of stopping short of the inevitable collision. But as it was, the trailer wheels caught the left front of my car, simultaneously crushing it and spinning me clockwise ninety degrees, depositing me in the ditch at a right angle to the roadway.

Marvelously, providentially, the farmer-owner of the semi was spraying his soybean crop in the nearby field, and promptly responded to the situation. Within what seemed only a minute or two, he appeared at the passenger side of my car and said "I've called 911. Hold on, the rescue team will be here in just a few minutes!"

The accident occurred only ten miles from my home base in Cooperstown, so the fire and rescue team arrived on scene promptly and went to work to extricate me. I was able to converse with them and suggest they cut the top off the car and pull me straight out the back, which they did. They covered me with a tarp and proceeded to carefully smash the windshield in preparation to remove the top. Once I was moved to the ambulance and then to the waiting helicopter airlift, the crushed vehicle could be hauled away. You can see the Alero resting on the collision center's flatbed trailer, its top resting on the engine compartment.

I would later show that picture to each doctor and nurse and therapist and visitor, evoking similar reactions from each one. They were collectively amazed that I survived the initial crash, let alone escape with relatively minor treatable injuries. The title of this work, "Three Feet from Death," comes from my own realization that, had I and my car slid another yard forward under those trailer wheels, the driver would surely have been crushed along with the engine compartment. I still shudder every time I think of that.

But I also marvel at the non-fatal outcome of this incident, and I contend that God supplied the grace, and the extra three feet of braking power, that saved me physically that day. Therein lies the primary miracle, the marvel I could live to relate. The ready response of the farmer and the rescue team, and the relatively complete recovery of which I can now write, are further evidence of God's handiwork.

The x-rays of my injury would reveal a fractured right tibia and fibula, and a severely torn left knee. Walking away from the scene would have been clearly impossible without an instantaneous healing of the sort only God can do. Just imagine if, by the time of the rescue team's arrival, I had gotten myself out of the car and begun to walk away from the scene without a scratch. Now there we would have a miracle on a plane with that of the paralytic to whom Jesus said, "Rise and walk," and the man was able to do so then and there. (Cf. John 5:1-9)

In the glossary of the Catechism of the Catholic Church we read this definition of miracle:

> "A sign or wonder, such as a healing or the control of nature, which can only be attributed to divine power. The miracles of Jesus were messianic signs of the presence of God's kingdom. (547)"[1]

We could argue endlessly over the difference between the kind of miracle that defies scientific explanation and the kind of extraordinary occurrence we might better term a marvel of divine providence. Nonetheless, I will accept anyone's assertion that "you are a miracle," because I firmly believe God intervened mercifully to spare me from death and provided the help I would need for rescue, treatment, recovery, and healing. That is miracle enough for me. With that understanding, I invite you to follow along with me as we walk through my experience and discover what we can gain from such challenging and traumatic moments in life.

---

[1]Libreria Editrice Vaticana, *Catechism of the Catholic Church (CCC)*, 2nd ed, English translation 1997, United States Catholic Conference, Inc., p. 888

2 Exaltation of the Holy Cross

The morning of Tuesday, September 14, 2021, dawned bright and clear with a crisp coolness typical of late summers in North Dakota. As scheduled, I was to offer a Mass at 9:00 am in the mission parish of Saint Lawrence in the small town of Jessie. I donned a light jacket for the twelve-mile drive from Cooperstown north and west to Jessie.

While preparing for the Mass, I noticed a shortage of the communion hosts we would need for the following Sunday. So, I resolved to bring some hosts following the Mass I would offer later that afternoon at the Parkview Nursing Home in Aneta, twenty-three miles northeast of Cooperstown. That decision could have proven fatal, as you will soon see.

Intriguing to note, September 14 is known in the Catholic Church and some other denominations as the Feast of the Triumph of the Holy Cross, alternately termed the Exaltation of the Holy Cross. I use the term "providential happenstance" to express my belief that God has a hand in circumstances that others might dismiss as interesting coincidence. By providential happenstance, then, this would be the day for me to take up the burdensome physical cross described in the following pages.

After morning Mass, I continued walking through the routine of the day as if it would be one like any other. I prepared my kit bag and vestments in readiness for the 1:30 pm nursing home Mass and loaded these into the Alero. The trunk was already filled with golf clubs, walking cart and other equipment, so I placed the Mass kit and vestments on the back seat atop other sundry items I hadn't cleaned out previously.

We have a nice little coffee shop, Nana's Café, in Cooperstown. Nana also serves lunch items. I stopped by in midmorning for my favorite brew and noticed the lunch special of the day was liver and onions. Such fare may not appeal to everyone, but I had not eaten liver and onions since my mother served it some thirty years before, and I thought it would be fun to try for old time's sake.

Pleasantly filled with liver and onions and chai tea, I set out for the Aneta Parkview Nursing Home. Mass went well with the dozen residents who joined me in the activity room for the service. Covid-19 virus distancing regulations were still in effect, so I was unable to join the residents in their dining room for coffee following the Mass. The activities director brought me cake and coffee which I consumed in silent solitude right there in the activities room. Pondering my next move, I resolved to return to Saint Lawrence Church and deposit the communion hosts I had remembered to bring along.

The rest of the day, to my mind, would be given to cleaning up the clutter in my Cooperstown rectory (parish house) in readiness for Mary Lou Hazard, our volunteer cleaner, who would be coming in the next morning. This was supposed to be a day like any other, unfolding according to my preconceived plan. Little did I realize what was about to happen. God had another plan for me on this Feast of the Holy Cross.

Cooperstown, Jessie, Aneta, and Finley, the communities I was serving, are all part of the agricultural heartland. Small grains, corn and beans and cattle are all raised in abundance there. Mid-September was the time of pinto bean harvest. Farmers these days usually use a chemical desiccant to dry the leaves and stems, making the beans easier to harvest. The large sprayers and the truck trailers hauling the chemical are actively working in the fields and traveling on the roads. From time to time there are unfortunate accidents involving such equipment. Mine was to be one of those.

I write the next chapter in the second person, as if you are now Father Dale Kinzler. I want you to experience, as fully as you can, what I went through that afternoon. Fasten your seatbelt, for you will need it!

3 Collision and Rescue

It is 2:45 pm on the afternoon of Tuesday, September 14. You have finished Mass and coffee at the Aneta Nursing Home. You have stopped by St. Lawrence Church in Jessie to drop off the communion hosts needed for the weekend Masses there. You close and lock the front door, then climb into the driver's seat of your Olds Alero. You have dubbed your vehicle "Olds Faithful" since it has served you well for over 275,000 miles.

You fasten your seatbelt, as has always been your habit, and turn the key in the ignition. You begin your eastward journey on North Dakota Highway 65, intent on making your usual right-hand turn onto ND 45 for the final seven miles of your southward drive to Cooperstown.

You have reached the highway speed of 65 miles per hour. Two miles east of Jessie you begin a gentle descent to a low spot in the road. There is a gravel road running north to south, and a stop sign at its intersection with the highway. You look to your left and notice a cloud of dust rising from the wheels of one of those farm trailers. It has been an unusually hot dry summer, so the dust is quite heavy. You assume the vehicle is going to stop as indicated.

Then your mental calculator does a split-second assessment of the truck's speed and distance from the intersection. Your heart leaps to your throat as you silently shout, "Oh my God, he's not stopping!" You experience an instantaneous rush of adrenaline and apply the brakes with all your might. Once you make that decision, taking the ditch to avoid a collision is not an option. The effects of a rollover could be worse anyway.

Your eyes grow saucer-size as your mind now silently screams, "IS THIS HOW I'M GOING TO DIE? LORD, I'M NOT READY!" You see yourself hurtling straight under the middle of the trailer, fully expecting to be crushed to death. But as it is, you have applied the brakes just soon enough and strongly enough that the trailer's rear wheels engage the front half of your engine compartment. You see those wheels acting as a trash compactor. Your adrenaline-fused system triggers your brain to watch all of this unfold as if in slow motion. You hear the crunching sound, and you see the engine collapse in front of you while you and your vehicle are spun clockwise and deposited in the ditch on the southwest side of the intersection. You see the safety glass of the windshield spider-web into a million tiny cracks though it remains intact.

Your Alero is tilted straight downward, perpendicular to the roadway. The front window pillars have collapsed along with the compaction of the engine compartment. Both front doors have popped open in the process. Your airbag has deployed, and the seatbelt has done its work. You were not thrown from the vehicle, but the centrifugal force has pushed you against the driver's door, lodging your left knee firmly under the arm rest.

You notice a pain in your right foreleg, and you suppose you have jammed your foot under the brake pedal in your desperate effort to stop short of the collision. You are unaware the passenger compartment has also compacted, fracturing your tibia and fibula, forcing the jagged edges of bone upward through your skin. This is the pain you feel as your brain attempts to assess the situation.

Your first thought is one of shocked surprise and gratefulness that you are still alive. But now you notice a few drops of blood on your left forearm from the blow to your cheek when the leftward momentum slammed your face against the driver's side door. Your breathing is labored, and you wheeze with a sound resembling the distant hee-haw of a braying donkey. Perhaps the impact of your chest against the steering wheel, or the dust particles from the exploding airbag, or the trauma itself, or any combination of these factors causes you to gasp for air.

Fortunately, by the grace of God, the farmer who owns the rig is spraying beans in the field nearby. Seeing the dust cloud and sensing the commotion, he brings his sprayer to rest on the highway and approaches the Alero. Leaning into the passenger side door, and seeing you are alive, he exclaims, "I've called 911! Hang on, they should be here in a few minutes!" He offers a bottle of water, and you graciously accept. The little sips offer some relief to your parched throat and help suppress your wheezing.

Amazingly, marvelously, the Cooperstown Fire and Rescue team covers the ten miles from town to the accident site within those few minutes. A half dozen men clad in their brown fire suits and yellow helmets with face shields begin their work. You recognize the faces of most of the men, members of your home community and even of the parishes you serve. One is president of our local bank. You are conscious enough to engage them in conversation. You tell them about your jammed left knee and your right leg that "feels like the foot is jammed under the brake pedal."

The ambulance soon arrives, and the crew is concerned about spinal injury. They apply a collar to your neck and advise you not to move. But you have already been moving your upper body a bit, so just after they apply the collar you cautiously move your head from side to side while muttering, “I – think – I’m – okay!” To help with your labored breathing, they apply a mask and administer supplemental oxygen.

Meanwhile Amy Fritel, one of our local nurses, happens to be driving northwest from Cooperstown to Binford, the next town west of Jessie. Coming upon the scene, she stops to see if she may be of assistance. She leans in, and recognizing you, announces, “Father Dale, this is Amy; you had our wedding!” You respond with recognition, “Yes, I remember.” “Are you going to faint?” she asks. “I don’t think so – oh maybe – no – maybe – no – maybe.” You momentarily slip in and out of consciousness about three times. You remain in a state of semi-conscious shock as the rescue effort proceeds.

Occasionally you look to your left and see the semi parked on the gravel road south of the intersection. You look to your right and observe a patrol car with the trooper standing outside. He is taking information and directing traffic while cars ease their way around the commotion. Your farmer angel is also assisting him in traffic control. He will later tell you that he saw your broken right leg when he leaned in to offer assistance and turned down your request to have him help you out of the car!

The ambulance crew says they will need to cut away your trousers so they can get you ready for the transfer. You comply with that, unaware of the fractured leg which they are going to stabilize. As professionals would do, they see the damage but do not tell you what they see. You would probably faint if you looked down and saw your injury, but the neck collar keeps you from doing that anyway. You reach into your right pocket and produce your wallet, remarking “We might need this for the insurance information.” You also gesture to the cell phone attached to the right side of your belt. You tell them you will want to be able to have that with you for contacting people about the accident.

You are alert enough to suggest the rescuers use their equipment to remove the top of the car and pull you out the back, since your left knee is pinned under the door handle and you "don't want to damage it any further." What you do not realize, though x-rays will later reveal, is that your ligaments and quadriceps tendon have all been torn, and there is a hairline fracture of your left pelvis. You have no doubt made the proper suggestion, and they will cooperate with you.

The men cover you with a blue plastic tarp and commence smashing the windshield. You watch thousands of tiny glass crystals fall onto the tarp. The men apply their saw to the window pillars, intent on removing the roof. You hear the rat-a-tat of the saw blades as they work. Though you are unaware of it at the time, you will later learn that it was your local funeral director who put the saw to work to extricate you from what could have been your metal coffin.

The men quickly and carefully pull you up and back out of the car and onto the ambulance gurney. While they are doing so, you cry out, "Oh, the leg! The leg!" They know of your injury but do the best they can to keep you calm. They tell you the helicopter is on the way from Fargo Sanford Hospital. You hesitate for a moment and ask them, "I am with the Altru System of Grand Forks and Devils Lake. Does that matter?" After a moment's discussion we resolve the issue, and you are assured Sanford will work with that. You consent to the air flight to Fargo.

You lie still in the ambulance for some ten minutes, waiting on the arrival of the Sanford airlift. The helicopter soon comes to rest on the roadway. Quickly and carefully, they transfer you to the chopper's gurney and slide you on board. Being pulled up and out of the Alero, and being transferred to ambulance and helicopter, are your most painful moments so far.

Soon you are aloft, and you listen to the copter's whirling blades while the paramedic on board attempts to start an intravenous port for the necessary medications and anesthetics. He is working on your right arm but having difficulty with insertion of the needle. You inform him your left arm has a wonderfully accessible vein, the one you have most often used to donate blood many times in the past. There he succeeds, and you are ready for the rest of the 100-mile flight to Fargo.

Your mind continues to race. You wonder if you are ever going to recover from the injuries you have sustained. You trust you are in the hands of a highly competent medical team, yet you wonder what all is going to happen next. You turn to God in prayer, using your fingers as rosary beads to recite that prayer you most often use when begging God for help in a particular need. Your own survival and recovery are your first and foremost intention this time.

Soon the air ambulance reaches the new Sanford Hospital in West Fargo and comes to rest on the helipad. You hear the rotary blades come to rest. The Sanford emergency team swiftly transfers you, albeit painfully once again, and wheels you to the emergency surgery room. The medical staff awaiting your arrival will now assess your wounds with MRI and x-rays, then prepare for the appropriate treatment. You are alive and in expert hands, praise God!

4 Saving Surgeries

From my cell phone information, the rescue team at the crash site contacted Greg Hazard, one of our Saint George Parish lay directors, who passed word on to our diocesan personnel. So, by the time they wheeled me from the helicopter into the surgery room, Father Phillip Ackerman, pastor of Holy Cross Catholic Church in West Fargo, was ready on site to administer the Sacrament of Anointing. Father Phil also received my cell phone and offered to take charge of contacting significant others via my string of recent text messages.

Drs. Anthony Brown and Benjamin Noonan introduced themselves. Dr. Brown would address my fractured right leg immediately and attend to the other minor lacerations. My left knee would simply be stabilized for later repair of the torn ligaments and quadriceps tendon by Dr. Noonan.

The surgery room clock showed 5:30 pm, the last I recall before going under anesthesia. It was remarkable to think that only three hours after the accident the Sanford surgical team was already preparing to work on my injuries. Thankfully there was no evident internal or spinal damage. X-rays did reveal a crack in my left pelvis, but that would require no surgery, only patience and time to heal. Of course, I could expect pain until that healing was complete.

Dr. Brown's surgical repair of the fractured right tibia would consist of a long rod inserted internally, fixed to the front of the tibia by screws at top and bottom to hold it together properly . The fibula would simply "come along for the ride." He assured me I would immediately be able to put all the weight I could bear on that leg and begin rehabilitation. This I found difficult to comprehend and emotionally accept. I could put no weight on my left leg though because the knee surgery would come a week later and require an extended time of healing.

The first hours and days after surgery were no picnic. Regaining consciousness in my hospital room, I noticed the clock now read 9:30 pm. Pains from the trauma, especially a throbbing headache, prevented me from sleeping a wink that night. It would be almost two days before I finally succumbed to sleep from simple exhaustion with the aid of a melatonin pill. Abdominal pains complicated the situation. Given my experience of a couple previous surgeries, recovery of bowel function was one of my main concerns. Senna and MiraLAX were prescribed for that purpose, but I grew impatient. Requesting a suppository and bedpan, I finally achieved the desired result. Sleep then came in fits and starts, an hour here, an hour there.

Soon began the flood of visitors, cards, and flowers. My brother Don had already been on scene while the Sanford crew prepped me for surgery. Brother priests began visiting in my hospital room the next day. One lady came in with a delightful array of flowers. "Do you remember me?" she asked. I replied she would have to help my aging memory. Identifying herself, she reminded me, "You had our wedding in Langdon in 1988." I was moved at the very thought of someone whom I served so long ago still appreciating me enough to come and visit. Seeking to recover my mental fumble, I quipped, "Oh yes, that was the Langdon Centennial year, wasn't it?"

The very next day, on Thursday morning, less than forty-eight hours after the accident, my case manager came in to announce there was an opening at the Post-Acute Medical Rehabilitation Hospital in Fargo, and I was a candidate for rehab therapy. Would I consent to the transfer? Dumbfounded at the suddenness of this proposal, I paused to ponder for a moment, then simply replied, "Sure, if you think that is best." The transfer would happen that afternoon at four o'clock. Hence my urgency about having a successful bowel movement, and my insistence on the suppository. It worked on time, and the transfer team was there on schedule.

Being moved from one place to the other was another adventure in the realm of pain and anxiety. At first, when asked to rate my pain on a scale of 1 to 10, I would bite my lip and mutter, "It's got to be at least a 9." But the staff were very kind, understanding my situation full well. Room 208 of PAM would become my home for the next month.

The flood of cards, flowers, and visitors would continue throughout that time. Our Bishop John Folda came to see me that first Saturday, and we had a very good conversation. My sister Charlotte from Mandan and her husband Terry Knittel, cousins from North Dakota and Colorado, current members of my Quad Parishes, previous parish members from Langdon and Fargo and Devils Lake, all came to extend their prayers and wishes. My priest fraternity prayer support group came over from their monthly visit in Fargo to spend the last couple hours of their day with me. I shared with them my vision of the Celestial Conference, about which I will write in the next chapter.

Deacon Wally Dalman with his wife Colleen, and Greg and Mary Lou Hazard came from home to bring my laptop, toiletries, some clothing, and a few other essentials. Marriage Encounter community friends Chris and Gina Ahlers came from their Fargo home to bring some useful hospital clothing, including a nice pair of warmups with generous legs to accommodate the medical hardware. Chris works at

Microsoft a stone's throw away, so he would come in with the daily paper. He even took me for a couple of wheelchair walks in the fresh air on the warm sunny afternoons of late September.

The main task during my time at the PAM Hospital was to begin recovery through rehabilitation therapy. Jonah, one of the physical therapists, introduced himself and took me to my first session. Soon he turned me over to Savanna, who took charge of the physical therapy on my legs. Ariana would work with me on occupational therapy, focusing on building arm strength to compensate for my compromised legs.

In another chapter I will share some highlights of the rehabilitation journey with its physical, mental, and spiritual challenges. But before that, let me share my initial pondering, the reflection I call the Celestial Conference, borne of my awareness God had done something marvelous in sparing me from death on the Feast of the Holy Cross.

5 Celestial Conference

On September 15, as I lay sleepless in my Sanford Hospital bed the morning after my initial surgery, I sought to mitigate the general pain and throbbing headache with stingily infrequent presses of the green self-administering medication button and began to reflect on my situation. Here I was, an accident victim who could have easily died just hours earlier. Had I and my Alero slid forward another three feet, I would most certainly have been crushed along with the vehicle. It was clear to me that merciful divine intervention spared me from death on the September 14 Feast of the Holy Cross.

Reflecting further, I realized that God must certainly have foreseen the collision. The decision, whether to "bring me home" at that point or let me stay on earth for a while longer, would be in divine hands. So, I let my imagination run with that thought. Come along with me now as I speculate on what could well have happened in heaven at that moment.

We of the Christian faith believe that God is eternal, and the heavenly realities are timeless. As is written in the Second Epistle of Peter, "With the Lord, one day is like a thousand years, and a thousand years are like one day." (2 Pt 3:8, cf. Ps 90:4) We measure the passage of time on earth, marking the days and months and years for the sake of reflecting on history, evaluating the present and anticipating the future. But God sees and holds all our earthly events in an "eternal now," as some theologians call it.[1]

At first, I thought of God working in a nanosecond during the millisecond my soul was silently screaming, "Is this how I am going to die? Lord, I'm not ready yet!" God can certainly respond that quickly and effortlessly, and I contend that God did supply that critical extra three feet of braking power, saving all but my lower limbs from serious injury.

Let's let our imaginations run a bit further and consider the possibility of a divine celestial conference with my significant others in the heavenly realm. Also, since God must have already foreseen the inevitable collision even two minutes or more before it happened, there was more than enough earth time to hold such a conference.

Who would be present for this saintly consultation session? No doubt my personal guardian angel. I love to contend that God has assigned two angels to guard me – one for the priestly activities of Father Dale Kinzler, and another for the man in all his athletic pursuits – both of whom I keep very busy! Those athletic pursuits will be covered in another chapter.

Then among my beloved personal saints, whom we acknowledge on All Saints Day, foremost would be my own parents, Howard and Mildred, who passed away within three months of each other in 2011, and whose bodies are laid to rest in the community cemetery of Alice, North Dakota. They were the original owners of the Alero and would have the greatest emotional investment in both me and that vehicle. I can well imagine God asking them if he should bring their son home now or let him stay, and I can hear Mom reply with her confident smile, "He will be with us soon enough," as Dad nods his head in agreement.

I have a great love of, and familiarity with, the deceased residents of that Alice Cemetery. Most all of mom's side of the family, the

Kapaun's and their other relatives, are interred there. I, myself, have purchased the plot where I will eventually be laid to rest, at the foot of my father Howard's grave. On occasion, while on my way to or from appointments in Fargo, I will pull off Interstate 94 thirty-seven miles west of the city and head south for nine miles on the road to Alice. There I will stop to pray at the cemetery in memory of all those relatives. I love to recite the five decades of the Rosary while walking among the graves of those family members I hope to meet in person once I pass away. My "Rosary Walk Among the Ancestors," I love to call this practice.

Most likely then, those family cemetery residents who also enjoy life in heaven would nod in agreement: "Let him continue to pray for us, and with us, and let us intercede with him for all who most need to benefit from his continued prayers and work on earth." Again, foremost among those clan members would be my second cousin, Father Neal Kapaun, another adventurous risk-taking fellow like me, who passed away many years before.

Let me tell you a bit about Father Neal. He was the son of my great uncle Ernest Kapaun, another industrious member of the clan, most noted for great work with orchard grafting in cooperation with North Dakota State University to produce winter-hardy fruit trees. Ernie and his son Neal loved to hunt and fish together. Neal developed great gardening and outdoor skills as well. As an ordained priest, Father Neal would apply his skills to such things as becoming scoutmaster of the local Boy Scout Troop of Wimbledon, ND, one of the parishes he served at that time.

My two years of summer scout chaplaincy at Camp Wilderness in 1970 and 1971 brought us into contact on those occasions when he brought their troop for their week of camping experience. Though

I was still unskilled in outdoor activities at that time, he clearly influenced me to try. He even invited me on two of the fall Canada fishing trips where he and his dad would camp out on one of the islands and catch as many walleye and northern pike as they could legally bring home.

Father Neal would send his annual Christmas letter to all of us family members. One year he reported his brush with death, when he and his car broke through the ice while on one of his winter fishing expeditions on an area lake. Fortunately, he had enough air left in the car while rolling down the window to equalize pressure, escape and swim his way to the surface. No doubt his two guardian angels were working overtime on his behalf that day!

Back to the main issue at hand, I credit Father Neal with favorable intercession on my behalf. In concert with him, the many other Kapaun and Wavra family members among whose graves I customarily walk, were there to register their approval. Joe and Ida Wavra Kapaun, my maternal grandparents, were certainly right there in spirit alongside Howard and Mildred, as are their bodies in the grave.

In case the Kapaun name rings a bell with our readers, I can affirm that we are also distantly related to Father Emil Kapaun, priest chaplain during the Korean War, whose heroic actions are now written up in his cause for canonization.[2] Perhaps Father Emil was also involved in this conference of family saints.

Although the decaying bodies of the deceased are separated from loved ones by death, I believe their immortal souls can easily meet in the timeless eternity of heaven at any given earthly moment. So let us also imagine that my sister Sharon and her husband Frank Hays and their son Bubba, and my mother's two sisters Florence and Lorraine, and their husbands Jimmy and Mac, all of whom have preceded me in death, were in on the conference at that moment. Their graves are as distant as Fort Sill in Oklahoma and Evergreen Cemetery of Colorado Springs. Add to that my paternal grandfather Charles Kinzler, buried in New Jersey where he had lived, and Grandma Hattie, buried in Lisbon after spending her last few years with us there in my hometown. Their bodies may be separated in death, but their souls are easily united in heaven.

I have little doubt that other priests and bishops I have known, and parish members whom I have served over some four dozen years of ministry, buried in a multitude of cemeteries, could all join the saintly assembly at that moment. Did God need to consult with any or all of them at that instant? Of course not. But I believe God still gives the saints of heaven some earthly good to do on our behalf. Saint Therese of Lisieux is known to have said, "I want to spend my heaven doing good on earth."[3]

And the Catechism of the Catholic Church attests:

"We believe in the communion of all the faithful in Christ, those who are pilgrims on earth, the dead who are being purified, and the blessed in heaven, all together forming one Church; and we believe that in this communion, the merciful love of God and his saints is always [attentive] to our prayers" (Paul VI, Credo of the People of God, 1968, §30).[4]

Here is one very clear and distinct instance where my personal saints must have all played a role in my amazing survival of the crash and the marvelous rescue. God did the divine work of the saving intervention, while they may well have been interceding on my behalf.

That pretty much sums up where my imagination took me while lying in medically managed pain in my Sanford hospital bed that first day. I had no dream of this sort, nor was I experiencing any kind of medicated hallucination. These were simply the musings of my meditative mind.

Let me clarify, also, that although I narrowly escaped physical death, I never had a "near death experience" in the classical sense of the term. My soul never left my body at any time during the accident and rescue. I saw no tunnel, nor light, nor angels, nor any saints, nor Jesus himself. Several months later, by providential happenstance, I met one lady who had such an experience, and in my brief conversation with her, she described the very kind of realities -- divine and angelic and saintly -- I have described here.

Celestial conference, divine intervention, and miracle of grace. I envision all these things working in concert. No doubt the Blessed Virgin Mary and her husband Saint Joseph, ready at the side of Jesus, stood front and center with the multitude I have just described. I can just imagine Mother Mary tugging Jesus' sleeve just as she did at Cana when she interceded on behalf of the newly married couple, "They have no wine." (John 2:3) She could just as easily have said at that moment on September 14 of 2021, "Father Dale is going to need help there quickly!" In the Rosary with which I am accustomed, we do, after all, ask her to "pray for us sinners, now and at the hour of our death." The prayer my own mother taught me, which she faithfully prayed every day, must have borne fruit on my behalf that day.

For the sake of any reader who is unfamiliar with this prayer, let me explain that the Rosary is not a magical mumbling or mindless rattling of beads. It is a meditative review of the mysteries of the life of Christ. Using an analogy from the world of music, I like to call the recitation of the five decades of the Hail Mary prayer the "repeating bass notes," while the mind focuses on the "treble clef," the primary notes conveying the melody of the mysteries of God's loving work through the life of Jesus Christ –Joyful, Luminous, Sorrowful and Glorious. It is meant to provide a fixed amount of time where we are praising God and interceding on behalf of any of our brethren in need anywhere in the world at that time. That is at least how I like to use the prayer.

I have little doubt that my Rosary Walk Among the Ancestors added weight to Mary's tug on Jesus' sleeve that day. The eternal Son of God, in harmony with the Father and the Holy Spirit, holds the divine power to work the miraculous things we experience here on earth. While not needing the intercession of the saints to do such divine work, it is in the heart of God to engage the whole Body of Christ in the signs and wonders God works here among us. I thank God for holding the celestial conference and sparing me from death until the "day and hour known only to the heavenly Father." (Cf. Mt 24:36)

---

[1] "As we see things naturally in the course of time, one event follows another and then passes into history. Not so with God. He lives, he is, an 'eternal now.' All that ever was and ever will be is present and actual in him now. It never ceases to have its full actuality. It is not past. It is not future. It is."

M. Basil Pennington, *The Eucharist Yesterday and Today* (New York, Crossroad Publishing Co., 1984), 40

Cf. also Peter Kreeft, ed., *Summa of the Summa* (San Francisco: Ignatius Press, 1990), 108: "We think of eternity as negative, as excluding time (for 'e-ternal' means, after all, '*not* temporal'); but in objective fact, God's eternity is positive and includes all times, for it can lack nothing actual, positive, and perfect that time contains. A remote parallel: the mind of an author contains, at once, all of his characters and the events of his plot."

[2]Cf. Roy Wenzl and Travis Heying, *The Miracle of Father Kapaun: Priest, Soldier, and Korean War Hero* (San Francisco: Ignatius Press, 2013), inside cover: "He was recently awarded the Medal of Honor, the nation's highest military award, and is being considered by the Vatican for canonization as a saint."

[3]St Therese of Lisieux, *The Final Conversations*, tr. John Clarke (Washington ICS, 1977), 102.

[4]CCC, §962

6 Rigors of Rehabilitation

It was Friday morning, September 17, the first day of waking up in Room 208 of my new temporary residence, the PAM Rehabilitation Hospital of Fargo. As required to qualify for the rehab journey of the next three to four weeks, I was contracted for two daily sessions in the therapy room. One session would be physical therapy for my injured right leg. There would be nothing for the left leg yet, other than to make sure I placed no weight on that foot for the next six weeks, to allow sufficient healing time for the surgically repaired tendon and ligaments. Dr. Noonan was to perform that surgery on September 22.

Jonah, the first physical therapist to meet me and accompany me to the therapy room, was pleased to see me insist on wheeling myself to the elevator and down the first-floor hall to our destination. The first session was a basic introduction to the process I could expect over the next three weeks. I would have physical therapy for right leg improvement in the mornings, and occupational therapy to strengthen my arms which would need to bear more than their usual load in performing daily tasks.

Savanna would patiently work with me on the leg, insisting I continue trying my best with each exercise. Ariana would work with me on occupational therapy for the arms. Those sessions would be much easier for me to face. The morning leg sessions were another story altogether. My journal entry reads:

I was overwhelmed with anxiety the first time she wheeled me to the ambulation track. There she coaxed me, and with mostly her strength, helped me stand upright, lock my arms straight on the parallel bars, and basically drag myself along for a half dozen painfully ugly steps. "Are you okay?" she asked. I nodded yes. She said, "Your face tells me otherwise." Then as I indicated I had had enough, her assistant backed the wheelchair up to me from behind, and with no effort to make a smooth transition, I plopped back onto the chair, an exhausted bundle of nerves.

Savanna noted the anxiety and said, "Next time we're going to have you take an Ativan ahead of time to help you relax." She was right. My brain was half the problem. It was telling me, "No way can you put full weight on this leg you fractured less than a week ago!" Mentally maximizing the physical pain, I dreaded those parallel bars.

But slowly, over the course of the next several days, Savanna pushed me to improve. Recumbent bike, weights and stretching, and practice standing, were all part of the training regimen. By the first of October she had me standing, with help, rising from wheelchair to walker and then stepping forward with the right leg. I was to be careful not to put weight on the left, which was fixed straight with a leg brace in locked position following the September 22nd surgical repair at Sanford Orthopedic Hospital.

My first steps were hesitant, very labored. My arms burned with the effort to bear most of the burden of my body weight. The assistant at my back measured the distance I covered. By Saturday, October 2, I was able to walk for two stretches, one measuring 55 feet and the next 64 feet. Being goal oriented as I am, I was determined to do a little better each time. I was learning the feeling of a heel plant and toe push-off once again. And I had donned

> a shoe, much more comfortable than wearing the hospital sock alone, which I had done on the parallel bars.
>
> I was proud and so grateful for these signs of progress, less than three weeks after my narrow escape from death. I knew the many prayers offered on my behalf were beginning to bear fruit.

I recall that first session on the ambulation track, when I could barely muster the courage to take my first step. I may have managed two, but that was it. With their help, I sunk back into the safety of the wheelchair, admitting momentary defeat. The remainder of that session consisted of some work with elastic weight bands and flexibility exercises. I saw several other people in the room, each working with their own therapist. Glancing over my left shoulder I saw an elderly woman enter the room, slowly pushing herself forward, hands on her walker. "Ooh," I sighed enviously, "If only I could do that!" My mind laid down the gauntlet, then and there. "I want to be able to do that by the time I am done here."

Sure enough, with Savanna patiently and persistently pushing me, with the aid of Ativan and my own self-prescribed dose of determination, I was able to pull myself along those parallel bars from start to finish, grimacing with each step. By the second week I was learning how to take my first steps with the walker, careful to let the left foot barely touch and bear only a minimal portion of my body weight. My left knee was now surgically repaired, the leg fixed straight in the brace provided. There would be no bending of that knee for the six weeks to follow.

My favorite therapy item was the exercise bike, where I could push the right pedal with my only usable leg. There at least I could feel like I was getting something resembling the old rigorous workouts to which I had grown accustomed over the years, and which I always assumed I would be doing well into my nineties, God willing.

By the third week they had me walking out in the hall, pushing myself through a marathon worth of effort, hands on the walker, left leg locked in the brace and admitting only a toe touch, right leg pushing itself through the pain for as many steps as I could muster before the assistant at my back would lower me into the waiting wheelchair.

Each day I would set a new personal best, forty and fifty and sixty steps. On the morning of the last day, just before my release, Savanna had me walk to a sport utility vehicle parked just outside and work myself onto the back seat where I could rest my legs and prop my upper body against the locked rear door. That was to be my graduation, advancing to home health care and outpatient therapy back in Cooperstown.

Meanwhile, back in Room 208, Ariana helped me learn how to slide out of bed and transfer to my wheelchair using the slide board. This involved another marathon's worth of determined effort on my part. But I did it in response to Savanna's instruction to the nursing assistants, written on the white board, "No more Hoyer!" I had relied on dutiful aides to transfer me from wheelchair to bed at night via the Hoyer lift, which one person could do without having to call upon a second.

Now I was to transfer myself from bed to chair, with belted assistance, and wheel to the bathroom. Once there, however, I still needed one or two assistants to help lift me up by the belt while I grabbed the safety bar, then help me swivel onto the toilet. Once I finished with the necessary duty, I would turn on the call light, and once again they would help me up to the bar while they completed the task of wiping. Holding onto the safety bar for dear life, right leg shaking like an aspen in the wind, left leg doing its best to remain unweighted, there was no way of wiping myself. This process I humbly accepted while feeling the helpless dependence of an infant. One of the nurses responding to the call reminded me, "The sooner you can put full weight on that right leg, the better it will heal. Stress on the bone promotes its healing."

I knew this, of course, from my years of running. I contend that my bones were denser than those of the average male of my age, thanks to the years of stress I had placed upon them with all my activity, as described in an upcoming chapter. Nonetheless, I was weakened both physically and mentally, lacking the courage to force myself to bear the pain, stand up straight and perform this task on my own.

Showering was another challenge, requiring Ariana's patient assistance. Wrapping my legs to prevent moisture invading the surgical stitches was an awkward project. She was very kind and respectful in working through the whole ordeal, doing her best to help preserve my sense of dignity and modesty. So too were the home health care nurses who would later help me through the same humbling ordeal twice weekly back home.

After twenty-one days of insurance-approved therapy at PAM, I was released for return to my home in Cooperstown. The Griggs County van supplied by the South-Central Transit Network was there, ready and waiting to accommodate me, my wheelchair, and my bundle of belongings. My mind raced with concerns for the recovery road that lay ahead of me.

Altru Health Systems of Grand Forks would provide home health care for me until early November. An occupational therapist also came to the rectory to continue working with me on prescribed exercises for both arms and legs. My left knee was still locked in straight position in the leg brace provided after Dr. Noonan's repair surgery of September 22. But by the first of November I could begin to let that foot bear an increasing share of the load.

A loyal parish volunteer came each morning to help me transition from bed to wheelchair. Leon Paczkowski would assist me, holding the chest belt as needed, and watch as I continued my quest for independence. I learned how to raise myself from the wheelchair and stand upright. I would position my nose in line with my knees and my toes, and strain to stand, hands and arms working overtime to liberate myself from the need of a helper. What a major accomplishment that was! I had practiced this maneuver at PAM but needed assistance to do it.

Now I could accomplish the feat on my own, and pace back and forth from living room to hallway to kitchen to laundry room and back. I would do this twice a day, once in the morning and once in the evening. Leon would return in the evening to assure my safety and assist me in the process of safely transitioning from wheelchair back into bed. At that point I was spending about twelve hours in bed and twelve hours in the wheelchair, with little breaks to stand and move about with the walker. I thought back to the day of my envious glance at the elderly lady that first day in therapy just six weeks earlier and breathed a prayer of thanks that I had progressed this far.

Next came outpatient therapy at the Cooperstown Medical Center. It was early November. Sarah Zorn and her support staff took over, guiding me through a disciplined regimen of exercises for strength and flexibility. At first, I could do very little with the braced left leg. Gradually we worked on unlocking the brace and flexing that knee. This was no picnic, to say the least. Degree by degree, session by session, we worked on increasing the degree of knee flex, in quest of the coveted one-hundred-thirty-degree bend. That would be one of our goals, along with gaining strength sufficient to walk independent of the walker and then to negotiate stairs.

Each session began with a warmup on the recumbent bike. That bike model simply required me to push the pedals back and forth with my knee brace unlocked, to begin gaining flexibility. It was my favorite part of the morning. The desk assistant would offer me coffee while I pedaled away for twenty minutes. Then came the rigors of therapy. Sarah had me try a cane for my first walker-free steps during the second week of November. I was so excited to discover my ability to take some fifty steps, with her at my side, while holding the cane in my right hand to complement my struggling left leg. In my Christmas letter to family and friends, under the picture of the therapist and myself sharing this triumphant moment, I wryly quipped "With Cane I'm Able!"

Later, Leon would bring me a recumbent bike from his home so I could practice in the rectory. The trouble is, this one required a full rotation of the pedals, a feat my stiff left knee could not yet accomplish. But I would move the pedals back and forth as far as I could, watching for every little bit of improvement I could muster. After about two weeks of this, I raised my arms in victory when I completed one full rotation of the pedals. Gaining confidence in the prospect of biking outdoors in the fresh air again, I slowly and carefully strained to complete yet another rotation, and another. Within a week I was recumbent cycling at the blistering pace of six miles per hour!

That homework, of course, set me up for more productive therapy sessions at the Cooperstown Medical Center. Our sessions, as allowed per insurance guidelines, continued until the first of April in 2022. On that last day, measuring the knee bend with her protractor, the therapist announced, "One hundred thirty-two degrees." From my supine position on the table, I shoved my arms into the air with a shout of victory.

I write a pastor's article for our local weekly newspaper, the Griggs County Courier, sharing that duty with three other members of our county ministerium, such that I write once a month. My article for January 7, 2022, entitled "The Better We Get," read:

> "The better we get, the easier it is to get better." This phrase came to me as I continue to mark my progress in recovery from my serious auto accident of September 14. Let me explain what I mean by it. My healing and recovery process continues to amaze me and those who are paying attention. After three weeks, when I was released from the Fargo rehabilitation hospital, I was barely able to shift from bed to wheelchair. With great effort I could rise to the walker and put weight on my right leg, dragging the left along with light toe touch.
>
> On October 28, I was permitted to put full weight on my left leg with its repaired quad tendon and knee ligaments. Suddenly new vistas opened up, and within a week I was doing walker-assisted walks of a half hour. Early in November, Sarah taught me how to walk with a cane. With guardian angels of the human kind at my side, I continued to practice that skill.
>
> On Christmas Day, I walked forward to the sanctuary with my quad-tipped cane and proceeded to celebrate Mass without the assistance of the walker. Sarah took me to the next level in the following therapy session, walking without the cane. We also practiced sitting and standing with legs only, no pushing off with the hands. This paves the way for going to the Activity Center for cardiovascular exercise and weight training. The better I get, the

easier it will be to get better. I can now hold out hope of resuming some of the activities, for which I am well known, by the time spring comes and the ice disappears. Easy does it of course, but each little victory spurs me on to set the next goal.

Now, I realize this is not true of all people, especially those with permanently disabling injuries. We may not have the ability to get better physically, and so may not be able to look forward to new horizons of physical activity. But all of us have a heart and mind and soul capable of getting better spiritually. I am finding, in my case, a renewed zest for prayer. I am taking the wake-up call of my accident as a reminder to give God first place in my life, and to be fully prepared for the day I am finally called home.

The decision for Christ, and the commitment to daily prayer and Sunday worship, are the first things that get us out of our spiritual hospital bed and help us to walk in the journey of salvation. A soul strengthened by the discipline of personal prayer, reading, and reflecting on the Scriptures and other sources of inspiration, will be better prepared to practice a lifestyle of Christian virtue. Strengthened by God's grace coming to our rescue in any trauma we experience, we become all the stronger for it.

Jordan Hoechlin is credited with this quote: "It never gets easier; you just get better." Having borne our share of Christ's cross, we are then graced to better live as God means us to do, to become 'another Christ' in word and deed. Our "inner Mother Teresa," as I like to call it, can begin to blossom. We can become the "best version of ourselves," as Catholic writer Matthew Kelly likes to call it. It is not easy to take the first stuttering steps, when we are not conditioned to do it. But the more effort we make to become spiritually conditioned, the better we become, and the easier it will be to get better, to keep ahead of those pesky sinful patterns that still nip at our heels as we run the course of life on the way to the finish line.

On our spiritual journey, we may at first make a few faltering steps on our own. But aided by the spiritual therapy of prayer and sacraments, the guidance we receive through the homilies at Mass or sermons in our place of worship, study of the Scriptures and teachings of the Church, we can continue to advance more readily in a life of virtue. The better we get spiritually through the practice of these disciplines of prayer, the easier it is to get better morally speaking, in control of our thoughts and words and actions.

My first workouts at the Cooperstown Community Activity Center were so uplifting and liberating. Carefully, strain-fully at first, I completed my first lap around the perimeter on the walking track. It would be twenty-two laps to the mile. Determined to give it a go for greater distance, I forged ahead, trekking poles in hand for assistance as needed. Forty minutes later I raised my arms in victory after finishing the full twenty-two laps, accepting praise and pats on the back from friendly bystanders.

Gradually, over the next several weeks, I would increase both pace and distance in my walks around that track. I would walk two miles and reach a pace of 18:30 per mile. That brought me the same sense of elation I experienced upon finishing the Ironman Triathlon in 1983 or crossing the finish line at the Boston Marathon in 1996 -- or finishing last in the Fargo 5k on Saint Patrick's Day of 2007 after my bunion surgeries of the previous November and December. (More on those in a bit.)

Trying the treadmill, I found myself still too unsteady to negotiate the moving belt without straining a muscle, so I left that machine alone in search of some other means of cardiovascular benefit. The elliptical climber became my friend for the next several weeks, as it continues to be. There I could reach maximal heart rate while climbing for a half hour at a pace of 120 to 140 steps per minute. With a couple minutes left to go I would grab the handles and hunch over like a cyclist racing to the finish line in a stage of the Tour de France, then ease up as I visualized myself passing the crowd of cheering onlookers at the finish. Seeking some spiritual benefit as well, while my body was engaged in the thirty minutes of climbing my mind paced itself through five meditative decades of the Rosary.

By mid-April the streets of Cooperstown were finally clear of the ice I so dreaded throughout the winter. The prime directive, "Avoid falling at all costs," had played loudly in my mind and kept me from any thought of walking outdoors. Finally, I could walk the same route I used to run, westward to our golf course and then northward on the road bordering the west side of the course.

In my pre-accident jogging days, I would turn around at the summit of a hill and complete a round trip of 6 miles, or 10k to be exact. Now I would walk just a couple of miles at first, but by mid-May that walk would stretch to the full 10k. I didn't care how long it would take, figuring God had loaned me the extra time to use and enjoy anyway.

Meanwhile there was the bicycle. So cautiously, ever so careful to guard the well-being of my weak left knee, I would mount my trusty Bike Friday (custom made folding bicycle) and give it a try. Like the experience of learning to walk again, the first efforts were scary but moderately successful. I managed to ride several blocks without falling, carefully planning to finish the ride with my right foot coming to rest on the pavement, absorbing the impact and sparing my weak left knee.

My goal was to join once again in the annual Newman Center fundraising bike ride at the end of April. I had been part of the first annual ride way back in 1986 while serving as pastor of the NDSU Newman Center and have participated in the event many times since then. As a matter of pride, determined to ride once more in 2022, I set my sights on that goal. Over the course of the years the ride directors had decided to shorten the race from its original distance of 37 miles down to a more manageable 25. This would make the goal much easier for a recovering cyclist to attain. This I did, accomplishing the task much slower than I would have done during my Ironman Triathlon years, but with equal elation.

"Are you fully recovered yet?" This question continues to visit me frequently in my conversations with acquaintances old and new. As of this writing I am saying "about eighty-five percent," realizing the ongoing difficulty with which I negotiate the challenging descent of a flight of stairs. I am not jogging, as I judge the left knee unable to sustain the impact of a running gait. But I am perfectly content to walk instead, while using the elliptical trainer for greater cardiovascular benefit. My knees will thank me for that decision because I continue to enjoy pain-free mobility, albeit at a slower pace. I can sit for longer periods with knees bent, without having to wince in pain. I can now complete a full genuflection at the altar at the beginning and end of Mass, a gesture of reverence I can proudly and gratefully perform once again.

My mantra, when first taking up my habit of jogging excessive distances, was "I am running now so that I will still be able to walk when I am ninety." In other words, let me keep moving and doing what I can to keep in better shape now, so I can still enjoy reasonable quality of life in my twilight years.

> "Though young men faint and grow weary, and youths stagger and fall, they that hope in the Lord will renew their strength, they will soar as with eagle's wings; they will run and not grow weary, walk and not grow faint." (Is 40:30-31)

In the next chapters I will rewind the tape of my past, to help you better understand the context of my spiritual reflections to follow.

7 Divinely Directed

"What made you decide to become a priest?" Many have asked me that over the course of the last half century. My tongue-in-cheek answer, but one well worth chewing on: "I didn't decide that; God decided it for me." A more thorough explanation requires the following abbreviated autobiography, in which I relate my awareness of the guiding hand of God in my life circumstances.

My parents, Howard and Mildred Kinzler, were long-time residents of Lisbon, North Dakota, a town of some 2300 residents. Howard, born in Philadelphia in 1915, was raised on the New Jersey coast and entered the Army Air Force to serve during World War II. Mildred Kapaun, born in 1917, was raised on a farm near Alice and received nurses' training at Saint John's Hospital in Fargo. They met while Howard was stationed at New York's Mitchell Field and Mildred had begun work in a hospital in Glen Cove, New York. They married in December of 1943 in Mildred's home church of Saint Henry's in Alice, North Dakota while Howard was on furlough. He would later be released from the war effort when their first two children, identical twins Shirley and Sharon, were born in February of 1945.

Howard and Mildred then moved to Lisbon where they managed the Fairway Foods grocery store originally owned by her industrious uncle Ernie Kapaun. Dale, that is I, was born in December of 1948. Later they would have two more children, Charlotte and Donald. We were raised in an environment of strong Roman Catholic faith, the religion of Mildred's upbringing. Howard, raised by devout Baptist parents, would eventually join us in practicing our Catholic faith for the sake of family unity in worship. We attended Mass at Saint Aloysius Church of Lisbon every Sunday without fail.

St. Aloysius Elementary School also provided the opportunity for a faith-based education, so mom saw to it that each of the five children attended there from first through eighth grade. By "providential happenstance," a new Catholic seminary high school opened in Fargo in 1962, the year of my eighth-grade graduation. I suspect that Bishop Leo Dworschak asked each pastor to recruit a candidate for enrollment in the class of freshmen who would be the first to attend the new Cardinal Muench Seminary. I was no doubt the most likely Lisbon prospect, being a regular altar server and the top student in my class academically.

Each year for eight years, the seminary added a class beneath us, so that by the time I completed college, the student body was comprised of the full complement of grades from high school freshmen through college seniors. The college seminary staff provided our religion, philosophy, and Latin courses, while North Dakota State University provided the rest of our college curriculum.

Free to major in the field of our choice, I took an interest in biology and earned a secondary education degree in the field of science, with a mathematics minor. I enjoyed the study of living things, from major ecosystems to microorganisms. They were for me a sign of the marvelous handiwork of our Creator. I also enjoyed mathematics from algebra to calculus, as well as the sciences of physics and chemistry. All these courses entailed the use of logic and reason to arrive at verifiable truths and demonstrable hypotheses. These disciplines appealed to me more than the subjects of religion and philosophy, which I accepted as part of the seminary requirements.

Father Ed Arth, rector of the seminary, assured me that if I continued to pursue the priesthood, I could most likely become the science teacher at the seminary in addition to offering the customary priestly ministry one would expect. With that assurance in mind, I could comfortably remain a seminary student while pondering the possibility of teaching science if I should for any reason decide not to seek ordination. Those were the years of the Second Vatican Council and the liturgical adjustments that followed soon thereafter. Along with another couple of classmates, I learned to play guitar and accompany some of the newly composed songs for our very first "folk Masses."

Graduating from Cardinal Muench Seminary College, I moved on to four years of major theology study at the Saint Paul Seminary of Saint Paul, Minnesota. Throughout those years I was still wrestling with my vocational decision, whether to become a priest or a science teacher. As God would have it, the choice for priesthood won out. It was a work of divine grace, I trust, that led me through the maze of my own self-doubts to the day of my ordination in Lisbon on June 2, 1974.

The events leading to that decision could be a story in themselves. In brief, I coasted through those years of theology without a sure sign of my call to priesthood. You might say I was following the road of least resistance, the academic life of excellence in studies with which I had been most comfortable for nearly twenty years.

By providential happenstance, while a theology student at Saint Paul, I landed a summer job as Catholic chaplain to the Boy Scouts at Camp Wilderness near Park Rapids, Minnesota. I had avoided joining Scouts during my boyhood in Lisbon, though my best friend Mike urged me to go along with him. I was too shy and too much of a homebody to do it.

But the Camp Wilderness chaplaincy would have me interact with scout troops and scoutmasters, watch them build fires and go on hikes. While providing two chapel services weekly, leading songs with guitar and preaching a sermonette at each service, I grew in confidence of my pastoral abilities. I also gained an interest in their outdoor activities. I would even help row the boat for the boys' mile swim merit badge. In later life I would begin to engage in those activities I missed in boyhood. I was a late-blooming Boy Scout, in effect.

After two summers as Camp Wilderness Catholic Chaplain, it was time to acquire more direct preparation for the work of priestly ministry. During the academic term of those same years, I was assigned to teach Confraternity of Christian Doctrine (CCD) classes at St. Joseph Parish of Hopkins, MN. I also played guitar and led songs at the Saturday evening Mass at St. Columba Church in Saint Paul. I experienced a semester of supervised CPE (Clinical Pastoral Education) at the University of Minnesota Hospital, practicing patient visitation.

Finally, after my third year of theology, in preparation for receiving ordination to the transitional diaconate, Bishop Justin Driscoll assigned me to a semester of ministry experience at St. Michael's Church in Grand Forks. There I would experience more of the workings of parish life.

One of the very significant experiences there was the weekly gathering of the Body of Christ prayer group. Through interaction with them, I began to grow in my own awareness of the love of Christ. A love of prayer, reading and meditation on the Scriptures, were the fruit of my participation with them. The matters of faith which I had treated as just another set of academic subjects up to that point were now the very subject matter I was being equipped to share with the People of God.

Gaining self-confidence and assurance that I was heading in the right direction, I could then move forward to my final pre-ordination retreat. During that experience I knelt before the tabernacle and held out my hands before the Lord in the Cardinal Muench Seminary chapel where I had attended so many Masses as a college student. With arms extended in a fashion resembling those of Jesus fixed on the Cross, I silently begged, "Lord, I am your problem. If I am supposed to become a priest, then I need you to give me the grace and strength I will need to do the work you intend me to do." I can look back on that moment now and simply affirm that Christ responded grace-fully to my desperate plea.

My years of priestly ministry began with two years each in Fargo and Grand Forks parishes. Then I was called into campus ministry for eight years at the St. Paul's Newman Center of North Dakota State University in Fargo, from 1978 to 1986.

Our next Bishop, James Sullivan, assigned me to St. Alphonsus of Langdon where I served for nine years until he called me back to the Nativity Parish in Fargo. From 1995 to 2007, Fargo would once again be my home.

The year 2007 was my twelfth at Nativity, and our diocesan Bishop Samuel Aquila determined it was time for me to move to another parish. We chose the city of Devils Lake, two-and-a-half hours northwest of Fargo. It was another relatively large parish with a Catholic School. I spent five enjoyable years there, but by the time of my 64th birthday I was beginning to suffer high blood pressure. After one scary fainting incident, my doctor determined it was time to begin medication with atenolol. Accepting a prescription medication was a new experience for me. I had been proud of my good health and the relatively healthy lifestyle I had maintained to that point.

Bishop Aquila and I mutually decided it would be in my best interest to take on a new assignment in a smaller community. So that is where I found myself from 2012 to the time of this writing, serving the rural quartet of parishes in Cooperstown, Jessie, Aneta, and Finley with a total of some one hundred fifty households.

The divine direction of the course of my life, as I see it, came through the circumstances moving me along the "road of least resistance" from childhood to the day of my ordination on June 2, 1974, in Lisbon, North Dakota. That direction continued through the authority of human instruments, namely the bishops who assigned me to the parishes I serve. There was no flashing light nor moment of instantaneous conversion, but simply the unfolding of the series of events which now, in retrospect, served as gradual revelation of God's plan for one Dale Kinzler.

"You formed my inmost being; you knit me in my mother's womb. I praise you, so wonderfully you made me; wonderful are your works! My very self you knew; my bones were not hidden from you, when I was being made in secret, fashioned as in the depths of the earth. Your eyes foresaw my actions; in your book all are written down; my days were shaped, before one came to be." (Ps 139:13-16)

Let's talk about titles for a moment. Most Catholics, and many Christians of other traditions, choose to call me Father Dale, or the more formal Father Kinzler. Other close friends and family simply call me Dale. When signing a check or other legal document, I will most often use the title Reverend Dale H. Kinzler. "Reverend" is more generally applicable to Christian clergy of any denomination.

I respectfully accept those who choose to call me Pastor Dale out of regard for the Scripture passage where Jesus says, "Call no one on earth your father, for you have but one father who is in heaven." (Mt 23:9)

I smile as I reflect on that passage myself. If I take it in the absolute literal sense, then I would be remiss to call Howard Kinzler my father as well. As I see it, Jesus is making the point here that we are all children in the one great family of God our heavenly Father. Howard and Mildred Kinzler, and I, and all of us, would acknowledge this when we say in the Lord's Prayer, "Our Father, who art in heaven." Yet we still use the terms "father" and "son" to identify our relationships with one another in our earthly dealings.

"Consider no one on earth your teacher, for you have one teacher." (Mt 23:10) In relationship to Christ, our great divine teacher, we are all disciples learning the way of eternal happiness. Yet when we sit at our school desks as students, we address that person at the front of the room as a teacher.

I do not shun the title, "Father," when addressed in the customary manner by anyone who does so out of respect for the position we hold. It means, after all, that the ordained priest is to bond with his people in a manner like that of the father of his household. Ours is not a biological, but a spiritual paternity. We are to give of our lives in service to the people entrusted to our care, much as the father exercises responsibility for his "domestic church" of husband, wife, and children. Each earthly father, biological or spiritual, should pray that we may serve as an image of the one heavenly Father whose love and providence grace us for our role of love and care in the global family of God's children.

With that understanding, let us continue our reflection on the day of God's merciful intervention, sparing the life of one Reverend Dale Howard Kinzler on the Feast of the Holy Cross. Before we do so, you will need to learn more about Dale Kinzler, the man and the athlete, and my unique experiences with some of the other autos I have driven.

8 Athletics and Autos

Before launching into further spiritual reflection on my experience of accident and rescue, I should lay more groundwork on my physical activities and travel habits. First the athletics, then the autos.

My thirtieth birthday was emotionally traumatic. The feeling of "going downhill" caused me concern about my physical condition. Though I had no major health issues, I wanted to do something to slow the inevitable decline I feared. I was the parochial vicar, or associate pastor, at the St. Paul's Newman Center of NDSU at that time. Noticing an advertisement for a lunch hour seminar on health and fitness on campus, I attended and followed up with a free assessment of body fat, lung capacity and other vitals. From there I registered for membership at the local YMCA and began running for cardiovascular fitness.

One day while jogging on the bike path accessible from the Y, I encountered one of the members of the Lake Agassiz Pacers Running Club. He invited me to join the long-distance training group that started from the Y each Saturday morning. Before long I was a regular participant in the weekly twenty-milers in preparation for an upcoming marathon race.

Although I failed to finish my very first marathon due to a dehydration collapse with less than a mile to go, I was hooked, and determined to succeed the next time. I became quite good at the event as time went on, usually finishing within the top ten percent of runners in the events I entered. Qualifying for the Boston Marathon was always a "carrot on the stick," but I never ran quite fast enough to meet the required standard for men in my age group.

Finally, at age 46, needing a time of 3 hours 15 minutes to qualify, I completed the Chicago Marathon in a very respectable 3:05. That was October of 1994, so I registered immediately for the next Boston Marathon. In April 1996 I joined 40,000 other runners for the prestigious 100th edition of that event. The hilly terrain of the last several miles caught me by surprise, but nonetheless a 3 hours 28 minutes finish felt very satisfying.

Bicycling had become an interest of mine as well. While serving at the Newman Center, I met some avid cyclists, members of the Great Plains Bicycling Club. Soon thereafter I invited one of the GPBC members and a builder of bicycles, to make me a custom racing bike with the latest Campagnolo components. Those were also the years when triathlon races were becoming popular. "If only I could swim better," I thought, "I would love to try one of those!" The YMCA pool was a handy place to improve my swimming skills and develop the endurance needed to complete the long distances the triathlon would demand.

Those who know me well are aware of my dogged determination to do the things my mind is set on. The triathlon became one of those fixations. Although the swimming leg of the event would always be my poorest, once I emerged from the water I was "home free." I would then catch and pass many in the biking and running portions, usually finishing somewhere in the middle of the pack .

My first effort at the Ironman distance Triathlon came in 1982. That event entails a 2.4-mile swim followed by 112 miles on the bicycle and concludes with a 26.2-mile marathon run. No, I never went to

Hawaii for their most prestigious Ironman event, but I found one more to my liking in Austin, Minnesota. That race involved a less intimidating lake swim, whereas I could never see myself swimming that distance in the ocean. Any degree of choppiness in the lake water would be risky enough for me.

As a matter of fact, I failed my first Austin Ironman attempt in 1982. The Minnesota air was only 57 degrees at the start of that late August event, and I went hypothermic 2 miles into the swim, with less than a half mile to go. I knew I was in trouble when my lungs started rattling, but I managed to dog paddle up to the next rescue canoe and tell them to take me in. On that day I could have died by drowning. With dogged determination, I resolved to work on my swimming skills and come back next year.

A serious triathlete must spend many hours training. The Newman Center's summer schedule of ministry events was quite relaxed, so I took advantage of the free time, spending the hours swimming, biking, and running. The Austin Triathlon was held earlier in the summer of 1983, thanks to their experience of nearly losing a swimmer or two in the cool water of the previous August! I was happy to finish the event in 13 hours, 45 minutes this time. But of course, I was determined to do better than that. More weight training at the YMCA, more swimming, and the new racing bike, led to a finish of 12 hours 25 minutes in 1984. Proud of that accomplishment, I saved my finisher's T-shirt to this very day.

By now you may be wondering what a priest is doing with such a focus on athletic achievement. Looking back on those years, I can ask myself the same question. I always justified my cardiovascular fitness pursuits with the belief that I was doing what I could to keep myself healthier for a longer span of years. I could then still serve the

People of God with better quality later into life. "I am running now because I still want to be able to walk when I'm ninety," I told myself.

There was a sense, though, in which running became my religion, as it were. During those years at the Newman Center, I would run nearly 365 days a year. I recall one day when the temperature was 20 degrees below zero and the wind was blowing some 20 miles per hour. I dressed in the appropriate number of layers, donned ski goggles to protect my eyes from freezing, and set out on an eight-mile run within the Fargo city limits. Just had to prove I could do it. Our running group called ourselves the Minute Men, ready to race a marathon at a minute's notice. Although I only entered one formal marathon race per year, I was *Semper Paratus*, always prepared, ever ready to run any distance any day.

Bicycling across the United States was another one of my dreams. Of course, I never had free time to do that, until the completion of my eight years at the Newman Center. In the spring of 1986, I already knew I would be transferring to St. Alphonsus Church of Langdon that July. I increased my bike training mileage to prepare myself for the cycle tour of my dreams.

By providential happenstance, Father Jim Ermer, then pastor of the St. Thomas Aquinas Newman Center at the University of North Dakota, in Grand Forks, organized a fund-raising bike ride whereby his students would gather pledges for riding from UND to the town of Hillsboro. He issued the challenge to us at the NDSU Newman Center, to gather students and raise pledges for riding from Fargo to Hillsboro, halfway between the two university cities. It was to be a friendly competition, serving as an incentive for all. We would meet at the finish line at the St. Rose of Lima Church in Hillsboro, share community lunch, compare numbers of riders and pledges raised, calculate finishing times of the ten fastest riders of each team, and declare a winner.

UND Newman Center was victorious that year, but I was clearly the "faster pastor." Already training for my trans-U.S. bike ride, I was in excellent condition. With smug arrogance, I declined the bus ride after the meal, turned right around and pedaled the thirty-seven miles back to Fargo, considering it a mere training exercise for the 3000-mile journey I was about to make before accepting my new parish assignment.

Being granted a month of vacation between assignments, I successfully fulfilled my dream that June. Averaging a hundred miles per day, I cycled eastward from Fargo to New York. From there I flew myself, my bike, and a duffle bag containing my panniers west to Seattle, then completed the return from Seattle to Fargo. Not only was that plan more convenient for its single flight arrangement, but I could also take advantage of the prevailing westerly winds for ease of cycling, with a homecoming welcome at the finish line back at the Newman Center.

Dream it, plan it, and do it. So many of my travels were like that. Camping and hiking were other interests of mine, fulfilling the dreams of this late-blooming Boy Scout. On occasion I have done brief hikes, in Glacier National Park and New England and Oregon. I hiked a portion of the Appalachian Trail, in fact one of the more challenging sections at Mount Washington, where I spent a hair-raising windy, rainy, chilly night in the middle of June. But I always had a hankering to become one of the through-hikers of that 2200-mile Appalachian Trail. The time that feat would require, however, would never be available to me until retirement. Nonetheless, that is exactly what I began to dream about. Can you sense my determination yet?

While serving as pastor of St. Alphonsus in Langdon from 1986 to 1995, I became friends with our local doctor, an Argentinian with a French wife. Marie-France taught French Literature at the University of Manitoba. As providential happenstance would have it, Henry and Marie-France Goodliffe invited me to vacation at their summer chateau in the foothills of the Alps in 1989.

Henry showed me a map of France and laid out a plan for me to fly to London with bicycle on board, take the ferry across the English Channel, and cycle tour the Normandy beaches, the Loire River Valley with its magnificent chateaus, then cross the Massif Central (much like our Appalachians) to their summer home. I had a month's vacation once more, with a priest substitute covering my Langdon Masses, so I could implement his suggestions. Dream it, plan it, do it. By this time, I was an experienced cycle camping tourist.

Once I reached their chateau, Henry let me take his Ford Pinto wagon to see the grueling Alpe d'Huez stage of the Tour de France bicycle race. That was the year our American Greg LeMond would win the event by a mere eight seconds in the final stage of the race, a time trial finish in Paris. It was exciting for me to watch all the big-name cyclists work their way up the hairpin curves of l'Alpe d'Huez. I had positioned myself where I could capture great photos of the competitors.

The very next day after that race stage, I drove to Lourdes, all the way from northeast to southwestern France. Reaching Lourdes after an overnight stop along the Autoroute, I parked Doc Goodliffe's Ford Pinto wagon beside a photo shop to purchase more slide film for my 35mm camera. By providential happenstance, as I came out and turned the key in the ignition, I was met with silence. The starter had failed then and there, after all the miles I had already driven.

Imagine what a predicament I would have been in if the Pinto had failed at the base of Alpe d'Huez!

I saw the hand of God at work in a subtly effective way. I had intended to make a simple stop and glance at the grotto of Lourdes, as if it were of no more interest than the many chateaus I had viewed along the Loire Valley, or perhaps Mont Saint-Michel, the island abbey on the Normandy seacoast. I would have spent no more time there than I had done in visiting the Normandy invasion sites of World War II, or the Bayeaux cathedral with its famed tapestry of William the Conqueror. I would have moseyed around the grotto property, taken in the sights to see, and moved on to the French Riviera. But providential happenstance would have none of that.

Pondering my predicament, I summoned enough vocabulary from my French lessons with Marie-France to dicker with the local garages, four of which declined to help. Finally, the fifth, the Citroen station directly across the street from the photo shop, would take it. *"Ce sera trois jours, monsieur."* With the weekend approaching, I could not expect the starter to be repaired until the following Monday. There I was, stranded with a mandatory three-day sentence in Lourdes!

Making the best of the situation, I took my bag out of the car, set up my little bike tent in the nearby campsite, and decided I may as well go visit the grotto. This is the place where the approved apparitions of Our Blessed Lady to Bernadette Soubirous in 1858 have drawn millions in pilgrimage every year. I made my way through the wrought iron entry gate and walked past the statue of Our Lady looking toward the Grotto Church.

Suddenly I stopped in my tracks. I thought I heard a voice. No, it was not an audible voice any bystander would hear. It was more like one of those "inner words" arising within the center of my own mind but originating from outside myself. The voice said distinctly as if it came through a loudspeaker, "YOU HAVE TRAVELED THOUSANDS OF MILES TO MEET ME HERE. I AM AS CLOSE TO YOU AS THE MOVEMENT OF YOUR HEART."

Jesus was reaching me, as was his Blessed Mother, with that all-important message of spiritual awareness. It was a subtly powerful and merciful wakeup call, reminding me to remember my priorities, my reason for being here. I had been all abuzz, scurrying about, accomplishing my own plan, doing my own will. For this moment in time my tour plans would be derailed in favor of spending time to reconsider my ultimate call, the purpose of my life journey. Resting where I was at, and letting my heart make that geographically imperceptible spiritual movement from closed to open in prayerful pause, would connect me with my ever-present, omni-present God.

"I AM AS CLOSE TO YOU AS THE MOVEMENT OF YOUR HEART." I would carry that mantra with me through the next marvelous three days of my "mandatory sentence" in Lourdes, and the rest of my journey in France, as well as my life journey to the present day.

That trip ended with a wonderful self-guided tour of Paris before flying home from London. I would go back once more, in 1996, to visit Henry and Marie-France and bicycle more of that marvelous French territory. But, by that time, I had taken on my next assignment, to serve the parish of Nativity in Fargo, with about 2000 registered households. Our ministry activities were abundant, and the staff was much larger than I had ever experienced previously. Parish responsibilities and our share in the Fargo Catholic Schools Network kept us pastors very busy.

Nonetheless I kept up my cardiovascular pursuits in a similarly vigorous fashion. Another feather in my athletic hat was my successful completion of the Pikes Peak Ascent race in Colorado Springs in 1999. In 2000 I returned and became one of the "doublers," completing the 13-mile ascent on Saturday and the 26-mile ascent/descent marathon on Sunday. As a faithful Catholic, I did go to church in Colorado Springs later that day, as a participant sitting in the pews, while my substitute was filling in for the Masses back home in Fargo.

I have never missed Mass while on vacation save for the one Sunday when I was in the middle of Pennsylvania Quaker country while negotiating my cross America bike ride in 1986. During my bicycle tour of France in 1989, the first Saturday evening of my week traveling along the Normandy coast, I found a church in the town square of the city of Fecamp. Ambling in with my cycling clothes, I took my place on one of the backless chairs. Intent on listening carefully to catch as much of the French as I could, I nodded off during the first reading and awoke to the sound of the people leaving the church at the end of Mass!

I can just imagine all the finger pointing I must have endured during that hour. After spending that night at the nearby youth hostel, I returned the next morning, found a laundromat near the church, and had clothes in the dryer while fulfilling my Sunday obligation, as I was determined to do. Though I did not preside at a Mass while vacationing in such fashion, I would never consider missing out on the Sunday gift of Holy Eucharist. I was determined to faithfully observe the commandment applying to us all, "Remember to keep holy the Sabbath Day."

In October of 1994, after completing the Chicago Marathon, I limped a couple miles to the downtown Cathedral and caught the noon

Mass, still clad in the warmup suit I had placed in my numbered plastic bag at the finish line before the start. Apparently, my odor was not unpleasant enough to prevent the lady in the next pew from approaching me to declare, "You have a nice voice. You should join our choir!"

My marathoning career ended in 2006, when I finally consented to surgical repair of bunion and hammertoe maladies. I successfully completed the first annual Fargo Marathon. But people were commenting on my noticeable limp, a condition I had steadfastly refused to acknowledge. Referred by my general practitioner to one of the best foot surgeons at Sanford Orthopedics, I presented myself for an evaluation. Dr. Richard Arness, upon reviewing the x-rays, was chuckling to himself. I asked what was the matter, and he replied, "You have been running with these? These are the worst I have ever seen!" He was referring to my misshapen toes, the source of my pain-induced limp.

Runners often learn to endure pain, and I had developed a high pain threshold in those three decades of running. With one foot repaired at a time, I was to keep each foot off the ground for a six weeks' period. From November to mid-February, I would have to manage with only one usable foot. I found the use of crutches unmanageable, so I purchased one of the earliest model knee walkers. This worked well for me. Never did I miss a day of ministry work. I would scoot from the Nativity rectory a couple hundred yards to our church and office during the whole three-month period. I enjoyed wheeling down the aisle and up our new handicap ramp into the sanctuary to celebrate Mass, one foot on the floor and the other resting on the walker.

One day I went outside to clear snow from the church sidewalk, pushing the shovel at right angles to the knee walker, using the walker for leverage. I hoped some compassionate soul would offer to take over the task, yet I didn't really want the help, for I needed to prove to myself I could do it. Stubborn-mindedly independent and determined, this old fellow was.

My most joyous racing event then came in March of 2007, when I completed the Saint Patrick's Day 5k race, walking those three miles on two newly repaired feet, finishing at the very back of the pack. The spirit of elation I felt that day would visit me once again when I walked my first mile following the horrific 2021 accident I have described. I would never run another marathon, although I did complete one or two half marathons in Fargo in 2013 and 2014. But I contented myself with cardiovascular maintenance runs in the five-to-eight-mile category, at a relaxed pace, enduring whatever knee pains and assorted minor injuries I would suffer as a result.

Autos

So much for my athletic endeavors and the level of fitness I enjoyed up to the day of my accident. Let's consider the demands of driving and the rigorous paces I have put my autos through over the past half century. My position as of this writing, serving four parishes encompassing 1,100 square miles in three counties, obviously entails more driving than if I were in Fargo, but I am quite used to sitting behind the wheel. I had logged well over a million miles in 47 years of priestly ministry to September of 2021 .

Before ordination, Dad let me use the family's 1968 Rambler American to drive to and from Saint Paul Seminary for my four years of theology. Upon ordination in 1974, he gifted me with a new AMC Matador. That vehicle gave me only 15 miles per gallon, and rising fuel prices forced my decision to purchase a cute little yellow

Honda Civic wagon in 1976. That vehicle lasted only 100,000 miles before it was puffing white smoke from the exhaust.

A 1984 Nissan Sentra wagon then served me for nearly 200,000 miles, followed by the 50-mpg 1993 Geo Metro I chose for even greater economy. By 1996, though, one of my fellow Fargo clergymen talked me into a deal on a used pearl-colored 1986 Audi in excellent condition, complete with spoiler and five-speed manual transmission. It was the sportiest and most solid car I ever owned, but I surrendered that to Father Joji, the visiting priest from India who worked with me for the year of 2002-3. A new 2002 Saturn would be next in my parade of vehicles. That one served me for yet another 200,000 miles.

In 2010, one of my Devils Lake parish members expressed interest in the Saturn with its manual transmission, a feature he found most appealing. So, I sold that to him and took advantage of the opportunity to acquire the 2004 Olds Alero owned by my parents. It would be one of my first automatic transmission vehicles. They had used it ever so gently, putting only 15,000 miles on the vehicle before entering the Lisbon Nursing Home in 2008-9.

The Alero ran so smoothly, I was determined to "drive it until it dies," even though I relegated it to second-vehicle status with the 2014 purchase of a sporty little red Chevy Sonic, using 40th anniversary gifts for the down payment. That Sonic survived nearly 200,000 miles before I traded it in on a gently used 2016 Chevy Trax. Its original owner had logged only 15,000 miles when I took it over in 2018.

I wanted to use the Trax much more sparingly and continue maximizing use of the Alero. By September of 2021 the Olds' odometer showed 279,000 miles of travel. I proudly dubbed the car "Olds Faithful." September 14 was to be another routine day of ministry and driving, a day like any other. But that was not in God's plan, as we have already seen.

9 Jinxed or Justified?

> "Therefore, since we have been justified by faith, we have peace with God through our Lord Jesus Christ, through whom we have access by faith to this grace in which we now stand, and we boast in hope of the glory of God. Not only that, but we even boast of our afflictions, knowing that affliction produces endurance, and endurance, proven character, and proven character, hope, and hope does not disappoint, because the love of God has been poured out into our hearts through the holy Spirit that has been given to us." (Rom 5:1-5)

The Theology IV class of Saint Paul Seminary in 1974 consisted of some twenty-five students from various dioceses around the country, mostly from the Upper Midwest. We were to be ordained in 1974. Most of us were ordained to the priesthood in our home diocese in early summer. My ordination, for example, was held on June 2 of that year.

David Gersch, studying for the Diocese of New Ulm, Minnesota, held off his ordination date until October 6. Sadly, shockingly, he died only four days later. October 10 was a rainy day, and he had stopped on the roadside to aid another stalled motorist. He was hit by a truck as he emerged from his car and was killed instantly. The online obituary reads, "During the late evening of October 10, Fr. Gersch was killed on a highway near Jordan, Minnesota by a truck that jack-knifed. He had parked his car to administer first aid at the scene of a multiple auto accident."

I had not attended his ordination but felt duty-bound to attend his funeral. It was a sad and shocking experience for me and all our classmates. Up to that time, the only funerals I had attended were those of my great grandmother and grandparents. The thought of losing a classmate and contemporary at 26 years of age was difficult to process. An icy chill gripped my being as I walked forward to view his body lying in the open casket at front of the church. His lifeless corpse was dressed in the vestments he would have worn only those few days from ordination to death.

It was difficult to comprehend how this sudden and tragic death could fit into God's plan for the life of Father David Gersch. Yet it is at times like this we most need to call upon God for grace to help us walk through such experiences together. Through the eyes of faith, we can look beyond death and burial to the eternal happiness of heaven God has in mind for Father Gersch and for all of us. Heaven would be the certain reward of this modern-day Good Samaritan.

This was not to be the last of the vehicle-related deaths of my Saint Paul Seminary classmates. Father Lloyd Janski was born on June 30, 1948, in Minnesota. He died on the 26th of December in 1981, my thirty-third birthday. According to the obituary, he was serving as assistant pastor of St. Peter's Catholic Church in Forest Lake, MN. From classmates I learned that his car was T-boned by a truck when sliding on an icy stretch of road during his return from visiting his parents in Waconia, MN for the Christmas holiday.

I was serving as assistant pastor at the St. Paul's Newman Center on the NDSU campus in Fargo at the time. Considering his funeral another must-attend event, I drove overnight to arrive on time for the 10 am Mass of Christian Burial in St. Peter's of Forest Lake. Once again, the icy chill of death prevailed on my senses, rivaling the

December chill of the Minnesota-Dakota winter. The faith-testing trauma of another death coming too soon and too suddenly presented a mystery difficult to solve. Was our Saint Paul Seminary ordination class of 1974 somehow jinxed?

I had laid those troubling thoughts to rest until my own serious accident of September 14, 2021. Had mine resulted in another fatality, we would clearly be far beyond the statistical average for traffic-related deaths in the general population. "Jinxed" is not a term we should be using as people of faith who look beyond superstition for answers to the mysteries of life. I would much rather, looking through the sharpened lens of faith, see these young men as "justified," having been cleansed of earthly fault and graced for early entry into their eternal reward.

I could still wonder about the jinx theory after reading of the vehicle-related death of yet one more priest contemporary. This one occurred only a month after my release from the PAM Rehabilitation Hospital. Picking up the October 28 edition of The Catholic Spirit, the weekly newspaper of the Archdiocese of Saint Paul-Minneapolis, I was stunned to read the headline on page 6: "Local Priest Dies After Being Struck While Riding Bicycle."[1]

The article began,

> "Father Dennis Dempsey, who served in the Archdiocese of Saint Paul-Minneapolis for 41 years, died Oct. 25 after being struck by a motorist in Rosemount while riding his bicycle. He was 73. According to a story in the Star Tribune, the motorist had been convicted 10 times for driving with a revoked license and may be charged in the incident."

The article goes on to note how Father Dennis loved kayaking, biking, and the outdoors. We would have been kindred spirits in that regard. Although he chose to wait until 1980 for ordination, I recall him well as another theology student at Saint Paul Seminary during my years there. His ministry of 41 years included many in the archdiocesan mission in Venezuela. He was obviously a well-loved and well-respected servant of the People of God through the gift of his many talents.

The article's concluding remarks from a co-worker express Father Dempsey's gift so well:

> "There's so many stories of Father Denny living the providence of God. However God allowed things to play out, he just trusted God . . . He trusted God in everything. That's what he taught us, really, is to just allow God to work in our lives and to trust God."

His obituary reads, "Beloved priest, avid outdoors man who loved biking, canoeing and hiking, died tragically on October 25 . . .Mass of Christian Burial Saturday October 30, 10:30 am at Church of the Risen Savior."

Had I been in suitable physical condition, I would most certainly have attended that Mass as well. But at that point the best I could do was pull myself into the back seat of a sizeable car and endure a short ride to my own mission churches to celebrate Mass from my wheelchair or a raised stool. Riding all the way to Minneapolis, some three hundred fifty miles away, was out of the question. I was able to converse with Father Kevin Clinton, another Saint Paul Seminary classmate, who gave the homily at Father Dempsey's funeral just as he had done for that of Father Lloyd Janski in 1981.

Father Clinton was so kind as to email a copy of the script of his homily, adding the comment,

> "For those of us who knew Denny, especially in recent years, the way he lived really challenged how we were living. The witness his "life-style" gave spoke volumes to me about what it means to have faith. Most of the content of my comments about each of the beatitudes comes from knowing Dennis and being a close friend of his. Many people who were touched by Denny's life knew exactly what I was saying about the beatitudes because that experienced what his life taught as well.

The Gospel reading chosen for Father Dempsey's funeral Mass was the familiar passage from Matthew 5:1-12, known as "The Beatitudes." So, for example, Father Kevin said,

> *[Blessed are the clean of heart, for they will see God.]*
>
> Oh, the freedom that goes with living simply. To not have a TV, yet be very aware of the important issues of the day. How free it is to be "OK" with the passenger-side car-door being able to open only from the inside
>
> and of course, never turn on air-conditioning—if it indeed works.
>
> To drive a car until it must be towed away for recycling.
>
> Oh, the freedom to use a flip-phone instead of the latest technology.
>
> How free it is to live simply so that possessions don't start possessing you.
>
> Oh, the freedom that comes to see God guiding and bringing all things to completion and just doing your part as best you can.

Here, then, was yet another example of our "jinxed or justified" priest contemporaries. Call it simply bad luck, call it the foibles of fate, call it unexplainably tragic misfortune, call it what you will. It could seem to us as if some sinister force was at work to undo the good our contemporaries would have otherwise done if allowed to go on living and serving in their respective assignments.

True, the devil could possibly be responsible for wreaking such havoc in our lives. A reflective reading of the Book of Job may refresh our awareness of this possibility. God may allow evil things to happen, confident that the goodness of the just person will prevail in the end. This is, after all, the primary lesson the Book of Job teaches us. Those who remain faithful to God will be rewarded at the end of the day, regardless of how much misfortune they may suffer in the meanwhile.

Where does that leave me, the exceptional one whose collision did not result in death? On the one hand I could feel guilty for surviving while other men of equal or greater holiness were taken. Who am I to deserve such a blessing? No goodness or merit of mine would earn such a favor. Several people have remarked, "Your work on earth is obviously not done yet." That message rings loud and clear for me as well. God obviously had a reason for sparing me that day. I contend he responded mercifully to my own micro-second plea, "I'm not ready yet!" and the intercession of those involved in the Celestial Conference of which I wrote earlier. Come to think of it, I wager that Father Gersch and Father Janski probably joined in that very conference.

In no way do I see myself more deserving of this extended earthly life than were Fathers David Gersch, Lloyd Janski and Dennis Dempsey. Our faith reminds us that God grants us many blessings we do not deserve. The gift of each day, and of all the time we may enjoy on earth, comes from the hand of a good and gracious God. Each person will experience God's grace in various ways, and we cannot measure our own blessings by comparing them to those of our neighbor. What he or she receives may well seem better or worse than what we receive.

I should neither grumble nor gloat upon comparing my relative health and length of life to that of my fellow human beings. I have no good way of knowing how well or poorly they are using the gifts they have. By analogy, we might think back to the Christmases of years ago when the family gathered around the tree to open presents together. For me, mom and dad always let us hint what we would like that year, pointing to the catalog page where the desired item could be found. Santa always came through, delivering as we hoped, request granted. Then I would learn what my friend got for Christmas, and feelings of jealousy would loom up from within.

Fighting off those jealous feelings, I could proceed to enjoy and use the childhood Christmas gifts I had received for the rest of the year. My friend could do the same with his gifts, greater in monetary value as they were. The level of joy I could experience with the solitary gift I had could well rival or exceed that of my friend. It is like that, then, with the many gifts of body and soul we are given over the course of our lifetimes. We may have more of one gift and less of another in comparison to our neighbor, but we can each enjoy and use well the gifts we have received from our loving God.

In sum, then, I am learning the lesson of living with my physical limitations, seeing them as gifts still to be treasured and used well, even if they may seem lesser in comparison to those I enjoyed in previous decades. I am still engaged in the process of seeking the "pearl of great price," the "treasure hidden in the field," which is worth selling everything else I have in order to obtain. (Cf. Mt 13:44-46)

When I lost my ability to run marathons, or even to run at all, I could still enjoy the capacity to walk. If I should lose the ability to walk in the future, I could still enjoy the capacity to think and to speak. Counting the blessings we still have, rather than mourning the loss of those we no longer enjoy, should be the hallmark of every person of faith.

The gift of longevity, then, is given to some but not to others. Although long life was considered one of the signs of God's favor in the Bible, it is not the ultimate. The Book of Wisdom seeks to help us grasp this truth:

> "But the souls of the just are in the hand of God, and no torment shall touch them. They seemed in the view of the foolish to be dead, and their passing away was thought an affliction, and their going forth from us, utter destruction. But they are in peace. For if before men, indeed, they be punished, their hope is full of immortality; chastised a little, they shall be greatly blessed, because God tried them and found them worthy of himself. (Wis 3:1-6)

> "The just man, though he die early, shall be at rest. For the age that is honorable comes not with the passing of time, nor can it be measured in terms of years. Rather, understanding is the hoary crown for men, and an unsullied life, the attainment of old age." (Wis 4:7-9)

Our length of life is not the final measure of its quality. Much like the men in the familiar Parable of the Talents, we will each have varying amounts of time entrusted to us, along with the various spiritual and material gifts at our disposal. The measure of our success, and the final determination of eternal reward or punishment, will hinge on proper use of our God-given resources of time, talent, and treasure. (Cf. Mt 25:14-30; Lk 19:11-27)

---

[1]David Hrbacek, *The Catholic Spirit*, October 28, 2021, 6

10 Conditioning Counts

Many who watched my rehabilitation and recovery process remarked how my good physical condition going into the accident must have helped me tremendously. I would affirm that observation, while issuing an even stronger affirmation of God's goodness and mercy at work on my behalf. This was a physical and spiritual experience, engaging body and soul in unison. My mental condition, spiritual readiness to accept whatever happens, and the determination to give my best effort also contributed to a better physical outcome than I might have otherwise experienced.

On the other hand, many who are in better physical condition than me have experienced more serious and more debilitating injuries from which they were unable to recover. This is understandable, unfortunate as it is. There is a kind of lottery factor in the arena of auto accidents. Some of us may escape relatively unharmed, while others are fatally injured. The accident victims have no say in the matter. We, and our family and friends, must play the hand we are dealt.

Physical condition is readily observable, and physical recovery is easier to chart. Mental and spiritual well-being is another matter altogether. I must admit that during my years of peak physical conditioning for marathons and triathlons, I was not paying enough attention to my spiritual health. While steadfastly running eight to ten miles a day, 365 days a year, I was largely neglecting the daily discipline of the

Liturgy of Hours -- the Psalms and Scripture readings prescribed for all priests and religious, available also to the laity. "Holy hours," periods of prayer and meditation before the Blessed Sacrament, were non-existent. I would celebrate the daily Mass with my congregation, and that served as my primary spiritual nourishment. But I contented myself with doing that and little more for spiritual conditioning.

The enthusiasm with which I had begun my priesthood was waning. My relationship with Christ, the love of God which carried me into the commitment to Holy Orders, was settling into a routine much like that of spouses involved in a mediocre marriage. .

My thirtieth birthday served as the mental trigger, the wakeup call, launching a new endeavor to preserve and improve my physical well-being and cardiovascular fitness. The accident of September 14, 2021, served as the wakeup call for a renewed endeavor of the spiritual kind. By analogy of the body, my soul had grown flabby with lack of exercise and preoccupation with material concerns. While this is not easy to admit, I would wager that many readers may find themselves in a similar spiritual condition.

Obesity, high blood pressure and clogged arteries spell trouble for our physical wellness. Fortunately, our medical professionals can readily detect these symptoms and offer therapeutic treatment designed to help us live longer with a better quality of life. We need to take advantage of the help they have to offer if we are suffering any of these symptoms. Spiritual obesity is not so easy to diagnose. Our spiritual heart may well suffer blockages due to a "poor diet" consisting of many influences running counter to Christian principle. Life stresses will "raise the blood pressure" of those who are not properly conditioned to handle them. The well-conditioned souls, on the other hand, will be better equipped for the rigors of the journey.

So, I simply acknowledge that God gave me a special opportunity to restore the balance of body and soul in my life priorities. May we not need such a drastic wakeup call to take our spiritual conditioning more seriously.

Granted, relatively excellent physical condition improved my prospects for recovery. If so, then it should also stand to reason that the well-conditioned soul will more readily rebound from the setbacks we encounter in our life journey. The soul fortified through regular prayer will be better prepared for the adversities we face while running the marathon of life.

Thankfully, whatever adversities I had suffered up to the time of the accident were relatively minor. God's grace was sufficient for me to persevere in each case. Tragedies within the family and conflicts within the congregations I served were manageable with help from above and from the proper human agents. So, I can confidently attest to the goodness of God at work within me.

Yet I am sure there could have been so much more fruit from my years of ministry, and no doubt God expected more of me over the course of those years. Each of us, looking back over the course of our lifetime, could probably say the same. In the biblical terms of the Gospel, those of us entrusted with five talents may have invested only one or two of them in service of the divine will. (Cf. Mt 25:14-30)

Christians have long debated the relative worth of good works in the salvation of the believer. Faith, as we know, leads us to accept the saving grace of God who takes the initiative in the great love relationship between the Lord and his people. Our response, then, is to "accept Jesus Christ as our Lord and Savior."

> "For, if you confess with your mouth that Jesus is Lord and believe in your heart that God raised him from the dead, you will be saved. For one believes with the heart and so is justified, and confesses with the mouth and so is saved." (Rom 10:9-10)

Important and crucial as that saving step is, it is but one leg of our ongoing journey of faith and salvation.

> "What good is it, my brothers, if someone says he has faith but does not have works? Can that faith save him? If a brother or sister has nothing to wear, and no food for the day, and one of you says to them, 'Go in peace, keep warm, and eat well,' but you do not give them the necessities of the body, what good is it? So also faith of itself, if it does not have works, is dead." (James 2:14-17)

The life we lead and the work we do in pursuing our commitment to Christ will condition our souls for the rigors of the race. Prayer and good work provide daily nourishment and the spiritual energy to continue our journey without collapsing before the finish line.

> "Do you not know that the runners in the stadium all run in the race, but only one wins the prize? Run so as to win. Every athlete exercises discipline in every way. They do it to win a perishable crown, but we an imperishable one. Thus I do not run aimlessly; I do not fight as if I were shadowboxing. No, I drive my body and train it, for fear that, after having preached to others, I myself should be disqualified." (I Cor 9:24-27)

11 Do This in Memory

Thanksgiving Day, November 25, 2021, was one of true thanksgiving for my second chance on life. Only two months before, I had experienced an amazing rescue on the day I was only three feet from death. Now I had already been presiding at weekend Masses since October 31, sitting at the altar on a raised chair and maneuvering about the sanctuary with my walker. Leon and Greg were taking turns driving me to the mission parishes of Jessie, Finley, and Aneta for Sunday and daily Masses. Daily Mass attenders were happy to have this opportunity after missing out for the six weeks of my absence.

On Friday, November 26, the day after Thanksgiving, Leon offered to accompany me on my first attempt to sit behind the wheel of my 2016 Chevy Trax and go for a drive. By then I could unlock my left leg brace and bend the knee just enough to work my way through the door, sit upright and place the foot of my "good" right leg on the accelerator. "Automatic transmission is a godsend," I thought to myself as I fastened the seatbelt and turned the key in the ignition. My right foot would be able to operate both the accelerator and brake pedal. Back in 2007, after my foot surgeries, I had to wait a full three months before both feet could manage their respective duties in my 2002 Saturn with its manual transmission.

Backing out of the garage ever so carefully, I eased the Trax into the street and worked my way south to the stop sign on Ninth Street, the main north-south road through Cooperstown. From the stop sign at Highway 200, I worked my way westward at a careful pace, gaining confidence as I moved along. Where should I go for this initial test drive? It took but a minute to decide on my route. I would turn north on Highway One and drive seven miles to its intersection with Highway 65. There I would turn east and drive through Jessie.

By now, Leon knew what I was up to. I would reach that low spot in the road, two miles east of the Jessie church, the same spot where I had narrowly escaped death on September 14. I had to leap the mental hurdle of re-living the moment of the crash. My jaw set rigid, my grip tightened on the steering wheel and my heartbeat quickened as I approached that unforgettable intersection of gravel road and highway.

I bit my lip and clenched my teeth as I passed, the crash replaying in my mind. I had to know I could once again negotiate that intersection safely. From that day forward I would look far left and right as I passed, making certain there was nothing coming. A good idea on any day, regardless.

We finished this maiden voyage by completing the rectangular clockwise route, turning south on Highway 45 back into Cooperstown where the highway becomes Ninth Street, made a right turn on Foster Avenue, and eased back into the garage. Mission accomplished. I would still accept rides in my volunteers' vehicles until the first of February, my self-declared Independence Day. By then I would be free of the leg brace and sufficiently mobile to walk to and from my car with the cane.

"Do this in memory." It became clear to me that what I was doing in re-living the moment of my accident each time I would later pass that intersection is analogous to the very thing we do in celebrating the Eucharist. We come to the altar in memory of Our Lord's Last

Supper, and we do this in memory of him, as he so instructed his twelve Apostles the night before he died.

> "Then he took the bread, said the blessing, broke it, and gave it to them saying, 'This is my body, which will be given for you; do this in memory of me.'" (Lk 22:19)

We say, in celebrating the Eucharist, that we repeat in an unbloody manner the once-for-all bloody sacrifice of Christ on the Cross on Calvary. Similarly, my encounter with that intersection replays in my memory, in an unbloody manner, the injuries I suffered on the bloody day of September 14. There is one vitally essential difference: mine is a memorial, pure and simple. There is no truck, no driver, and no collision, thankfully, only an imaginary one.

Eucharist, on the other hand, is living memorial and true sacrifice, in which the same Christ who died on that cross is really and truly here for us each time we consecrate the elements of bread and wine at the altar, repeating Christ's words, "Take and eat, for this is my body," and "Take and drink, for this is my blood."

> "The cup of blessing that we bless, is it not a participation in the blood of Christ? The bread that we break, is it not a participation in the body of Christ? (I Cor 10:16; cf. also I Cor 11:23-26)

Continuing my reflection on this analogy, I celebrate three Masses per week, on average, at the St. Lawrence Church in Jessie – one on the weekend and two during the week on Tuesdays and Thursdays. I must admit to rushing to arrive in time to begin promptly as scheduled. Punctuality is one habit I have yet to master, and it is not one of the post-accident fruits I have gained. Therefore, on many days I may pass that infamous intersection with hardly a passing thought of the events of September 14.

Is that not like our all too frequent experience of the Mass? Our minds may be far adrift with the many concerns of the day, and we are physically present but mentally and spiritually absent. No accusations here, other than a challenge to myself, to be more intentionally focused on what I am doing at the altar as I preside. I have established some checkpoints at which I stop during the liturgy to ask myself, "Am I still here?"

Marvelous to say, the miracle of transubstantiation -- whereby the elements of bread and wine, whose "accidents" or visible and tangible characteristics remain the same, are changed in substance, or nature, to become the "Body and Blood, Soul and Divinity" of our risen and glorified Lord Jesus Christ -- does not depend on the mental state of the presiding priest. The proper recitation of the words of institution, by the duly ordained and authorized priest, suffices to invoke the power of the Holy Spirit and effect that marvelous transformation, the miracle performed by God himself.

As our Catechism of the Catholic Church affirms,

> "At the heart of the Eucharistic celebration are the bread and wine that, by the words of Christ and the invocation of the Holy Spirit, become Christ's body and blood. Faithful to the Lord's command the Church continues to do, in his memory and until his glorious return, what he did on the eve of his Passion: 'He took bread. . . .' 'He took the cup filled with wine. . . .' The signs of bread and wine become, in a way surpassing understanding, the Body and Blood of Christ; they continue also to signify the good of creation."[1]

As a priest entrusted with the awesome privilege of presiding at the celebration of Eucharist, I beg Our Lord to help me, "Father Dale 2.0," to pray with greater focus, and greater devotion, as I do this in memory of the Last Supper and the redeeming sacrifice of Calvary.

And may the Church, our People of God, the mystical Body of Christ called to holiness, do the same.

> "I urge you therefore brothers, by the mercies of God, to offer your bodies as a living sacrifice, holy and pleasing to God, your spiritual worship. Do not conform yourselves to this age but be transformed by the renewal of your mind, that you may discern what is the will of God, what is good and pleasing and perfect." (Rom 12:1-2)

---

[1]*CCC*, 1333.

12 Solidarity in Suffering

I find in the human heart and soul a natural tendency to feel compassion toward others who suffer. It also seems natural to identify with them, and to reflect on our own experiences of suffering, however light or severe they may be in comparison.

For example, let me share a few of the cards I received during my period of hospitalization and rehabilitation. Everyone who sent a card was aware of the accident and the amazing fact of my survival. They may or may not have known the exact nature of my injuries. But several chose to relate a time where they, too, experienced some sort of injury.

Judy Jacobson of Fargo wrote:

> "It is a miracle that you are still alive, God was not ready for you yet. Same as for me, our job down here is not finished yet. My accident was in 1992. I was coming back home from seeing an elderly woman as I was working in home health for the county. I got caught in the gravel that was plowed to the side of the county road, lost control and tumbled down a steep hill. I hit a tree which pushed the driver side of the car halfway across the steering wheel, fracturing seven ribs and causing a bad head injury. Keep working at rehab; you will do great!"

I was later able to converse with Judy, whom I also knew as a member of my former Fargo parish of Nativity, when we met at the fundraising banquet for our Real Presence Catholic Radio station in February of 2022. She readily acknowledged divine intervention sparing her from death in that incident, much the same as mine.

Judy Zimprich, member of St. George in Cooperstown, wrote:

> "I empathize with your injuries from an accident in 2005 – pelvis, ACL, PCL, tibial fractures, etc. I was just listening to a song, 'Angel Armies,' and the God of Angel Armies is definitely on your side. Your angels surely protected you from other injuries!"

Elaine Hill, a member of my former parish of Langdon, wrote:

> "I'm so glad to hear you're getting along okay. I'll keep you in my prayers. I'm kind of home bound as I have macular degeneration and can't drive anymore. So, my outings are to church and doctor appointments. I'm so lucky to have Holly across the street. She picks me up for Mass on Tuesdays and Thursdays. Also, thankful my son and daughter-in-law are in town."

Elaine would pass away just a year afterward. God grant her eternal rest.

Sister Michaeleen Jantzer, OSB, then at age 92, a co-worker during my years at the NDSU Newman Center, wrote:

> "Many of us continue to pray for you to heal from your injuries. I am still here at the Estelline Care Center (South Dakota) still not able to walk. I need to use a wheelchair to get around. I have not given up hope of walking again. I have seen another doctor but still have no answers. Thanks for your prayers. May God continue to heal you."
>
> In a later card she wrote, "This past week the doctor told me there is little hope that I will ever walk again. I continue to pray for your healing."

I replied to Sister Michaeleen, writing,

> "I am sorry to hear you are unable to walk, relying on the wheelchair to get around. It reminds me the ravages of age will one day overcome us all, even if accidents do not! I may tuck this wheelchair of mine in the closet for possible use a couple decades down the road as well, should God happen to grant me that many more years."

I later learned that Medicare was renting the wheelchair on my behalf but had not purchased it, and I therefore did not own it. So, I returned it in February when it was clear that I no longer needed one for the foreseeable future.

My heart goes out to the permanently disabled, or rather, let us call them the physically challenged. Disability is a relative term, subject to prejudicial judgment. Take for example the many accident victims whose injuries result in permanent paralysis. Yes, they suffer serious limitations of their physical abilities, yet they often rise above those limitations in other ways. Consider the paraplegic or the double amputee, who cannot run the Boston Marathon as those of us with two normally functional legs might do. But it is amazing to watch the wheelchair marathoners push themselves along with strong arms and cross the finish line with amazingly impressive times. Witness the multitude of athletes who participate and excel in the Paralympics.

These are exceptional individuals, of course, and the average person relying on a wheelchair may never enjoy such accomplishments. Yet they are still capable of great things. There are so many wonderful employment opportunities for those who can work at home or in an office, where their hands and their minds might well outperform the work of the physically advantaged.

I go for annual eye checkups with a doctor who wheels himself into the room and performs all the needed tests while seated in his wheelchair. He is a fellow car accident survivor. The condition of his legs has no bearing on the quality of his work. He has, no doubt, had to work harder than others to earn his credentials and gain his place among the eye professionals in the state. We have conversed on life interests and hobbies, sharing a mutual love of golf. He had been a very competent golfer before his accident, and still golfs with a specialized cart to assist him. It helps stand him upright so he can take a stance and swing the club with sufficient success to still enjoy the game.

Throughout the course of my injury, rehabilitation, and recovery process I found myself temporarily identifying with the many levels of physical handicap others experience as permanently challenging. For forty-eight hours I lay in the hospital bed in Fargo Sanford, essentially paraplegic and racked with pain. I could readily identify with the many who are bedridden and in need of nursing assistance for the most basic functions of feeding and bathroom care.

Upon my transfer to the PAM Rehabilitation Hospital, I found myself in solidarity with the many who are permanently wheelchair bound, though my use of wheelchair would last merely another four or five months. I would spend half the day in bed and the other half in the wheelchair, either in my Room 208 or down in therapy sessions. As described earlier, I needed assistance transferring from bed to wheelchair and back, and extra help with bathroom functions. I felt helpless and guilty for imposing on the overworked staff to help me into the bathroom, to clean me up and get me back to the wheelchair when finished.

I can hardly imagine what it is like to require that level of assistance for the rest of one's life. But that is exactly what we see in our nursing homes and extended care facilities throughout the land. I have gained much greater compassion for our elderly and permanently handicapped people, and much greater respect for their caregivers, through this experience. I will never forget the gracious aides who responded to my nighttime call for assistance in transferring back into bed. If only one person was available to help, I recommended they use the Hoyer lift, much easier for one to operate, I felt. But Savanna would soon forbid its use, knowing I should be capable of more.

I will never forget my first encounter with the walking track in the therapy room, where I failed to manage even one or two painful steps, my arms stiffly supporting me, frozen in place on the parallel bars and struggling just to remain upright. With the assistant behind me clutching the belt around my chest, I slumped back into the wheelchair in defeat. As a consolation prize, we moved on to some easier work with the elastic bands. It was then I glanced over my left shoulder and spied the elderly lady entering the room with her walker. "Ooh, if only I could do that!"

Every day now I encounter people, younger and older, who need the aid of their walker to ambulate from place to place. I found solidarity with them during my second and third weeks at PAM, as well as the next several months at home. Though I was capable of fifty or sixty steps by the time of my homecoming, it would not be long before the onset of winter, with the snow and icy streets and sidewalks typical of North Dakota from late November to mid-April. That meant I would be a shut-in until spring. Here again, I found solidarity with the many who may be ambulatory but choose to stay indoors for fear of falling and breaking a hip or a limb during those slippery months.

And, of course, I could not drive myself while in this condition. I felt solidarity with all those who have lost their independence, relying on others for transportation. I was so grateful for my parishioner volunteers who drove me to my mission parishes for Mass, from late October through February. But in the meantime, I agonized over the limitations restricting me to the most essential travel while my remaining vehicle, the Chevy Trax, sat unused in my garage.

Certainly, I could have easily felt compassion for others without having suffered my own accident. But now I felt a genuine solidarity with the permanently disabled, in a way I could not otherwise do. Searching my inmost thoughts, I realized I had always subconsciously placed myself above those who suffered such misfortunes and limitations. I was, after all, the paragon of endurance and physical fitness, presuming I would continue my regimen of activities well past my eighties and into my nineties. In that nearly fatal moment of the crash, my tower of superiority came tumbling down.

Reflecting upon my newfound humility, I realized this experience brought me into a deeper kind of solidarity with Jesus Christ, our Suffering Servant. At this point I thought it best to check some higher authorities for the theological points I am considering here. So, I consulted one of the works I had already set aside shortly after the accident, when making the decision to write: the 1984 Apostolic Letter of Pope John Paul II, "On the Christian Meaning of Human Suffering" (*Salvifici Doloris*.)[1]

Karol Wojtyla, now known as Saint Pope John Paul II, is considered one of the most brilliant and articulate philosophers and theologians of the century. His letter on suffering is replete with reflection on the relevant Scripture passages that help us find positive meaning and value in the suffering we encounter.

John Paul II begins his Apostolic Letter with the Scripture reference from Paul's Letter to the Colossians:

> "Declaring the power of salvific suffering, the Apostle Paul says: 'In my flesh I complete what is lacking in Christ's afflictions for the sake of his body, that is, the Church. Now I rejoice in my sufferings for your sake.'" (SD 1, quoting Col 1:24)

Paul's quote is controversial, and not readily understood without explanation from worthy commentators. The Passion, Death and Resurrection of Christ suffices to redeem all sinful humanity – past, present, and future. This is the clear and constant teaching of every Christian perspective. There is, in that sense, nothing lacking in what Jesus of Nazareth did through his suffering. But, as Paul infers, what is yet lacking is our own entry into that saving action, applying its grace to our own journey of salvation.

I liken it to the analogy of electricity. Jesus' sacrifice on the Cross of Calvary is the source of all the "spiritual electricity" available to mankind always and everywhere. We, simply and necessarily, must plug our own spiritual lamp into the available socket in order to "live in the light," as it were. John Paul's use of the term "salvific suffering," then, does not mean our suffering saves us or merits eternal life per se. It simply means, as I see it, that my suffering is a means of plugging into the one Source of grace flowing from that eternal Sacrifice of Christ.

The concept of salvific, or redemptive, suffering was not new to me. Christ redeems us, we do not redeem ourselves. But our individual suffering helps us turn toward the merciful Redeemer for the saving grace flowing from that all-sufficient Sacrifice.

I had read and pondered and preached on the value of our suffering on many occasions through the years. But now it was time to put theory into practice in my own life. If this newfound suffering brought me into spiritual communion with my suffering brothers and sisters, then it also brought me into deeper union with Jesus Christ. That being the case, I realized I should embrace rather than rue the suffering this accident brought on.

The Son of God freely chose to enter the sphere of human life, taking on the condition of our mortal flesh, including its proneness to pain and suffering. His is the supreme example of solidarity with the children of God, becoming like us in every way save for sin. From his agony in the Garden of Gethsemane to his last labored breath on the Cross, he endured a level of pain and suffering few of us could tolerate. Granted, the duration was relatively brief, but the impact of this ultimate sacrifice of the divine Son in obedience to his Father is eternal.

> "The witnesses of the New Covenant speak of the greatness of the Redemption, accomplished through the suffering of Christ. The Redeemer suffered in place of man, and for man. Every man has his own share in the Redemption. Each one is also called to share in that suffering through which the Redemption was accomplished. In bringing about the Redemption through suffering, Christ has also raised human suffering to the level of the Redemption. Thus each man, in his suffering, can also become a sharer in the redemptive suffering of Christ." (SD, 19)

This is another complex statement, calling for considerable explanation. To put it as simply as I can, in my own words and that of theologians, we realize that Jesus' redemptive sacrifice, offered on the Cross of Calvary, is sufficient for the salvation of all, as was said above. Our personal suffering serves as a means of entering into, and sharing in, that once-for-all sacrifice of Christ. And, as John Paul uses the term "man" in the inclusive sense of "humankind," we realize that every human being is included as a subject of Christ's Redemption.

"Raising human suffering to the level of the Redemption," then, in effect, means that our suffering brings us, and people of every century in human history, to the foot of the Cross of Christ, where we may also hear the words he uttered, "Father, forgive them, they know not what they do (Lk 23:34)." And, like the repentant thief hanging on the cross beside him, we may hear him tell us, "Amen I say to you, this day you will be with me in Paradise (Lk 23:43)."

"Thus each man, in his suffering, can also become a sharer in the redemptive suffering of Christ." Here again, we are not "saving others" as if we do the work only Christ as God can do. But we accept his saving grace through these ways of "taking up our cross to follow him," and we may also give witness to others who suffer, prompting them to follow in the footsteps of Christ, shouldering their crosses as well.

While writing this chapter, by providential happenstance I stumbled upon this prayer from the Evening Prayer of the Liturgy of Hours for that day:

> "Father, precious in your sight is the death of the saints, but precious above all is the love with which Christ suffered to redeem us. In this life we fill up in our own flesh what is still lacking in the sufferings of Christ; accept this as our sacrifice of praise, and we shall even now taste the joy of the new Jerusalem."[2]

Returning to the Apostolic Letter, "On the Christian Meaning of Suffering," I reviewed the entire document and will highlight a few of John Paul II's major assertions, to enrich our understanding of the place and the value of suffering in our lives. Following are my summaries and a few relevant quotations from the document:

In his section titled "The World of Human Suffering," John Paul notes that our suffering, a universal experience of human life, has both a physical and a moral dimension, as well as a social and interhuman dimension:

> "The world of suffering possesses as it were its own solidarity. People who suffer become similar to one another through the analogy of their situation, the trial of their destiny, or through their need for understanding and care, and perhaps above all through the persistent question of the meaning of suffering." (SD n. 8)

Beyond the kind of suffering one individual may encounter, there is that of a whole population:

> "Natural disasters, epidemics, catastrophes, upheavals and various social scourges: one thinks, for example, of a bad harvest and connected with it – or with various other causes – the scourge of famine. One thinks, finally, of war." (SD, 8)

His Holiness names the two World Wars, and especially the Second World War, bringing a "great harvest of death" and a heavy "burden of human sufferings." Added to that is the threat of nuclear war and the possible self-destruction of humanity.

In his next section, titled "The Quest for an Answer to the Question of the Meaning of Suffering," John Paul II affirms our Christian understanding that, while God is a "just judge who rewards good and punishes evil," yet our suffering is not simply equated with punishment for sin. Job, for example, was a just man who is "aware that he has not deserved such punishment, and in fact he speaks of the good that he has done during his life." From the beginning of the book of Job "it is apparent that God permitted this testing as a result of Satan's provocation." (SD, 10-11)

Further, "Profoundly rooted in the entire Revelation of the Old but above all in the New Covenant" is the redemptive aspect of suffering: "Suffering must serve for conversion, that is, for the rebuilding of goodness in the subject, who can recognize the divine mercy in this call to repentance, . . . to strengthen goodness both in man himself and in his relationships with others and especially with God." (SD, 12)

The next section, titled, "Jesus Christ: Suffering Conquered by Love," serves as the crux of his presentation (pun intended). Citing that most quoted verse of John's Gospel, "For God so loved the world that he gave his only Son, that whoever believes in him should not perish but have eternal life," (Jn 3:16), John Paul notes that "these words, spoken by Christ in his conversation with Nicodemus, introduce us into the very heart of God's salvific work. They also express the very essence of Christian soteriology, that is, of the theology of salvation." (SD, 14)

Clarifying what Jesus means by the word "perish," he writes,

> "Man 'perishes' when he loses 'eternal life.' The opposite of salvation is not, therefore, only temporal suffering, any kind of suffering, but the definitive suffering: the loss of eternal life, being rejected by God – damnation. The only-begotten Son was given to humanity primarily to protect man against definitive evil and against definitive suffering. The mission of the only-begotten Son consists in conquering sin and death. He conquers sin by obedience unto death, and He overcomes death by His resurrection." (SD, 14)

While we usually associate the suffering of Christ with the events of his Passion and Death, the Holy Father broadens our awareness:

> "Christ drew close above all to the world of human suffering through the fact of having taken this suffering upon His very self. During his public activity, he experienced not only fatigue,

> homelessness, misunderstanding even on the part of those closest to Him, but, more than anything, He became progressively more and more isolated and encircled by hostility and the preparations for putting Him to death." (SD, 16)
>
> …"Precisely by means of His cross He must accomplish the work of salvation. This work, in the plan of eternal Love, has a redemptive character."

The Apostolic Letter's next section, titled "Sharers in the Suffering of Christ," asserts: "Every man has his own share in the Redemption. Each one is also called to share in that suffering through which the Redemption was accomplished." (SD, 19)

Now we recognize the great diversity of forms of human suffering, and the varying levels of intensity we may experience. In the example of my car accident, I was fortunate to survive with very treatable and relatively temporary injuries. Thousands of accident victims are much less fortunate, given the statistics on fatalities issued each year in our country. That leads to the suffering of the survivors, multiplied many times over in the grief of loss of loved ones.

Addressing the pain of loss we suffer in the passing away of our beloved family and friends, John Paul cites the second letter to the Corinthians:

> "For this slight momentary affliction is preparing for us an eternal weight of glory beyond all comparison, because we look not to the things that are seen but to things that are unseen." (2 Cor 4:17-18)

Now he places his opening reference to Colossians in context:

> "Now I rejoice in my sufferings for your sake, and in my flesh I complete what is lacking in Christ's afflictions for the sake of his body, that is, the Church." (Col 1:24)

He continues with a reflection on the Church as Body of Christ, in which "Christ wishes to be united with every individual, and in a special way He is united with those who suffer." And while Christ has accomplished the Redemption, "even though it was completely achieved by Christ's suffering," this Redemption "lives on and in its own special way develops in the history of man. It lives and develops as the Body of Christ, the Church, and in this dimension every human suffering, by reason of the loving union with Christ, completes the suffering of Christ." (SD, 24)

We have then, as John Paul notes in his next section, a "Gospel of Suffering." The reality of human suffering now takes on a positive dimension in its salvific character:

> "Christ did not conceal from his listeners the need for suffering. He said very clearly: 'If any man would come after me … let him take up his cross daily.' (Lk 9:23) (SD, 25)

Christ prepared the many followers who would suffer persecution on account of their faith in him, and their witness, even to the point of martyrdom, inspired others to take up their cross in turn. Then there are *those for whom suffering an injury or loss becomes the occasion of a* conversion (italics mine.) John Paul cites the example of St. Ignatius of Loyola, a soldier who began reading the Bible during his period of hospitalization following such an injury.

> "When this body is gravely ill, totally incapacitated, and the person is almost incapable of living and acting, all the more do interior maturity and spiritual greatness become evident, constituting a touching lesson to those who are healthy and normal." (SD,26)

In the final section, titled "The Good Samaritan," John Paul highlights this parable and its importance in the Gospel of suffering:

> "For it indicates what the relationship of each of us must be toward the suffering neighbor. We are not allowed to 'pass by on the other side' indifferently; we must 'stop' beside him. Everyone who stops beside the suffering of another person, whatever form it may take, is a Good Samaritan. The name, 'Good Samaritan,' fits every individual who is sensitive to the suffering of others, who is 'moved' by the misfortune of another."
>
> …"Nevertheless, the Good Samaritan of Christ's parable does not stop at sympathy and compassion alone. They become for him an incentive to actions aimed at bringing help to the injured man. In a word, then, a Good Samaritan is one who brings help in suffering, whatever its nature may be." (SD, 28)

With this condensed summary of the Apostolic Letter, we come full circle to the concept of solidarity in suffering. My own suffering instilled in me a greater sense of compassion for others who find themselves in similar situations. I, in turn, found myself the "victim fallen by the wayside" who became the occasion for many other Good Samaritans to step in and offer their assistance. They were able to step in and walk alongside me, and even help carry the load of my cross, during my own little climb of Calvary, as Simon of Cyrene did for Jesus.

As I wrote this chapter, I realized God was giving me an unmistakable confirmation of the reason my accident occurred on September 14, the Feast of the Holy Cross. I wager every reader has come to the same conclusion.

---

[1]Apostolic Letter of His Holiness Pope John Paul II On the Christian Meaning of Suffering, *Salvifici Doloris*, St Paul Editions, February 11, 1984

[2]Liturgy of the Hours, Week 3, Sunday, Evening Prayer I

13 Chastening Chastisement

God uses trouble to pave the way for something greater.

> "For I know the plans I have for you, declares the Lord, plans for welfare and not evil, to give you a future and a hope." (Jer 29:11)

> "Endure your trials as 'discipline': God treats you as sons. For what 'son' is there whom his father does not discipline.... Besides this, we have had our earthly fathers to discipline us, and we respected them. Should we not then submit all the more to the Father of spirits and live? They disciplined us for a short time as seemed right to them, but he does so for our benefit, in order that we may share his holiness. At the time, all discipline seems not a cause for joy but for pain, but later it brings the peaceful fruit of righteousness to those who are trained by it. So strengthen your drooping hands and your weak knees. Make straight paths for your feet, that what is lame may not be dislocated but healed." (Heb 12:7-13)

Consider the weather, for example, as subject matter for a reflection on the trials we face. We all know well enough the damaging effects and severities of the storm kind, be they hurricanes, tornadoes, blizzards or what have you. Does God, cloaked as "Mother Nature," send these catastrophic weather events as punishment for the sins of humankind?

Being a lifetime resident of North Dakota, I have endured three-quarters of a century of challenging winter weather. I began writing this chapter in December of 2022, when my home community of Cooperstown, like most of our state, had already seen snowfall amounts rivaling some of our severest winters on record.

Oh yes, I can recount the great blizzard in March of 1966, watching from the third story of Cardinal Muench Seminary as the fellow in the neighboring house dug down to reveal the rooftop of his automobile buried under the snowdrift. Thirty years later came the nearly 100 inches of snowfall in 1996-7 leading to one of our worst floods in the history of the Red River Valley. I was in Fargo helping my brother Don sandbag and took his family into our rectory for a month while their home was inundated with water above the level of the first floor. Meanwhile, the city of Grand Forks was totally flooded, lost power, and then fire broke out in the downtown area from the disastrous combination of water and downed power lines. The Grand Forks Herald published its iconic headline article on April 21, 1997, "Come Hell and High Water."[1]

The cleanup and recovery efforts were daunting for communities up and down the valley. But it paved the way for future flood control efforts and better preparedness.

In 2022, Cooperstown had its first wintry blast on November 6 and 7, followed by frustratingly frequent intermittent light snowfalls, such that we seemed to be shoveling every other day. By Thanksgiving Day, we were remarking, "It seems like it has been a long winter already, doesn't it?" Then on December 12 through 15, dear Mother Nature unleashed a statewide winter storm resulting in school closures and no-travel advisories for the four-day period. Blizzard conditions continued for the next three days, as blustery winds blew the snow back onto roads already plowed and sidewalks already shoveled. I did not drive anywhere save for the weekend Masses in our mission parishes on roads decently passable, thanks to our dedicated highway crews.

During this weather event I would initiate banter with friends and neighbors by slyly remarking, "Boy, the people in Arizona just don't know what they're missing. They could be enjoying days like this!"

Thankfully, I have parish volunteers who do the lion's share of snow removal. But I have done my share of shoveling by hand, one scoop at a time. I have a little mantra I frequently mutter under my frozen breath: "Penance for the remission of sin." You may laugh at that and think it archaic or even slightly heretical. We are saved from sin by the death and resurrection of Jesus Christ, so none of our penitential works or sacrifices purchase saving grace, correct? I am not suggesting we are saved by our snow shoveling. Catholics, like all Christians, recognize that Christ's sacrifice on Calvary is the once-for-all redeeming sacrifice. Yet Christians also consider it important to engage in penitential acts of some kind, uniting ourselves with the suffering of Christ as we do so. Lent is one season where we specially focus on the penitential aspect of the Christian life.

With each shovelful of snow, rather than grumble against God and/or Mother Nature, I choose to turn it to a prayer. I want to consciously praise God for the privilege of another day to face whatever challenges it brings, including the weather I will experience, be it hot or cold, wet or dry. As I scrape the sidewalks, I can offer a prayer for those who have not the strength to lift a shovel. I can intercede for those who have no home in which to shelter themselves from foul weather. And I can turn to our loving and merciful God in repentance for all my past sins which may well deserve a chastisement greater than a few inches of snow to shovel.

The harsh winter continued relentlessly all the way through April of 2023, resulting in many days of school closure, canceled activities, and missed Masses. Late crop planting was another inevitable result. In May of 2023 we were rewarded with warm weather, well above normal. Of a sudden, we were begging for rainfall. Such is the unpredictability of our local weather.

The whims of Mother Nature are but one dimension of the unpredictability of human life. The dangers inherent in driving are another. We can never know the day nor the hour when a vehicle collision may interrupt our plans to reach our destination safely. So too, our journey of health care and physical maintenance entails many unforeseen calamities. One never knows when a heart attack or stroke, or cancer, may be lurking just around the corner, waiting to strip us of our bodily well-being. And then we have the ever-growing risk of attack by a robber or terrorist.

Should one of these invasive events befall us, we need not question whether God has sent it our way as punishment for our own misdeeds. Jesus addressed this very concept by using an example from the news of a misfortune in his own day:

> "At that time some people who were present there told him about the Galileans whose blood Pilate had mingled with the blood of their sacrifices. He said to them in reply, 'Do you think that because these Galileans suffered in this way they were greater sinners than all other Galileans? By no means! But I tell you, if you do not repent, you will all perish as they did! Or those eighteen people who were killed when the tower at Siloam fell on them – do you think they were more guilty than everyone else who lived in Jerusalem? By no means! But I tell you, if you do not repent, you will all perish as they did.'" (Lk 13:4-5)

Most notable in our own generation would be the tragic events of September 11, 2001, when the terrorist attack on the Twin Towers in New York and the Pentagon caused the loss of 2,996 lives – 2,977 victims and the 19 hijackers who committed murder-suicide.[2] Those falling towers were the result of an evil act perpetrated by malevolent individuals who acted clearly against the will of God. I steadfastly contend that Allah, as Muslims name the One God, was not pleased with the terrorists' actions, regardless of how convinced they may have been of the righteousness of their own mission.

I should not step out on my own theological limb here, on a most sensitive matter touching upon both the religious and political realms. I cede, therefore, to the more carefully couched language of the United States Catholic Conference of Bishops:

> "Any simplistic connection between Islam and terrorism must be rejected. The most effective counter to terrorist claims of religious justification for violence or, for that matter, to those who claim that religion is mostly a source of conflict comes from within the world's rich religious traditions and from the witness of so many people of faith who have been a powerful force for non-violent human liberation around the world. September 11th presents a challenge to the Church as well as our government to come to a deeper level of understanding and engagement with Islam."[3]

No one who died in New York or Arlington or in the downed airliners that day was being singled out by God as deserving punishment. In my perspective, they are modern day martyrs for having been slaughtered by misguided Islamic extremists. I contend those 2,977 victims would be numbered among the sheep of Matthew's judgment scenario while the 19 suicidal terrorists would be relegated to the fate of the goats. (Cf. Mt 25:31-46)

But then, I should not be the one to judge, as that is finally left up to God. No one can know the state of soul for each of the victims, so we cannot pronounce them all saved for that matter, either. It would have been up to each of them to be "ready and watchful" for the day of the Bridegroom's arrival in preparation for the wedding feast. (Cf. Mt 25:1-13) Nor should I render final judgment on the perpetrators of the attack. Who can know for certain what they encountered on the instant of facing death, and whether or not they repented of their misdeed in that final moment?

> "Stop judging, and you will not be judged. Stop condemning and you will not be condemned. Forgive, and you will be forgiven." (Lk 6:37)

So then, neither should we judge our God, or place God on trial, as it were, for allowing these things to happen. Granted, given the lot of sinful humanity, we may well deserve whatever chastisement comes our way. But, as our previous chapter's reflection on human suffering reminds us, such misfortunes are part of the predictably unpredictable nature of daily taking up our cross and following Christ.

Our calamities may serve as an occasion for us to rise above them and renew our resolve to "strengthen our drooping hands and weak knees," and set our feet on the straight path of holiness.

In my own case, I accept the consequences of my accident, the pains of injury and the rigors of rehabilitation, as an extended opportunity to do "penance for the remission of sin." It could certainly be a well-deserved chastisement. But I prefer to embrace its chastening after-effect, namely the greater resolve to balance my priorities and to prepare more earnestly for the life to come. God must love very much this son whom he has so disciplined.

---

[1]https://www.grandforksherald.com/community/from-the-archives-come-hell-and-high-water-25-years-ago-the-flood-brought-some-of-its-toughest-days

[2]https://en.wikipedia.org/wiki/Casualties_of_the_September_11_attacks

[3]https://www.usccb.org/resources/usccb-response-september-11

14 Created for Crosses

Did Jesus Christ really need to be crucified in order to redeem us? This is arguably the most challenging concept in the message of Christianity, and one of the most difficult for us to embrace and apply in our own life experience. Wouldn't there have been some other way? And how can a good God allow so much suffering in our world and our lives?

My September 14 accident, sustained on the very day our Catholic liturgical calendar observes the Feast of the Exaltation of the Holy Cross, led me to ponder this Christian mystery more deeply. Being three feet from death, and living through the after-effects of the accident, is certainly the most challenging cross I have borne up to this point in my life. Other crosses of the physical kind, in fact, have been relatively minor by comparison. My narrow escape from death was both physically and emotionally traumatizing. While working my way through the pains of healing and the challenges of physical therapy, I identified more closely with Christ on the Cross of Calvary than ever before.

Ironically, or rather by providential happenstance, as I like to call it, it was fully fifteen months later when I chose to write this chapter. On the morning of December 14, 2022, I paused to pray the Office of Readings. These words from the pen of Saint John of the Cross, whose feast is observed on that day, caught my attention:

> "Would that men might come at last to see that it is quite impossible to reach the thicket of the riches and wisdom of God except by first entering the thicket of much suffering, in such a way that the soul finds there its consolation and desire. The soul that longs for divine wisdom chooses first, and in truth, to enter the thicket of the cross. Saint Paul therefore urges the Ephesians not to grow weary in the midst of tribulations, but to be *rooted and grounded in love, so that they may know with all the saints the breadth, the length, the height and the depth – to know what is beyond knowledge, the love of Christ, so as to be filled with all the fullness of God.*
>
> The gate that gives entry into these riches of his wisdom is the cross; because it is a narrow gate, while many seek the joys that can be gained through it, it is given to few who desire to pass through it."[1]

This reflection from John of the Cross echoes the very words of Christ himself:

> "Enter through the narrow gate; for the gate is wide and the road broad that leads to destruction, and those who enter through it are many. How narrow the gate and constricted the road that leads to life. And those who find it are few." (Mt 7:13-14)

This is not a numerical prediction, as if to imply that most people will wind up in hell and only a fortunate few go to heaven. Rather, we understand it as meaning that we must, in that sense, go against the grain, move upstream against the downward current of the world, head into the wind, and counter the gravitational pull of a godless worldview.

The concept of the necessity of suffering may be a bitter pill to swallow, especially for those immersed in the pursuit of a pleasure-oriented lifestyle as their ultimate ideal. We are, indeed, created for happiness, as our Catholic Catechism affirms:

> "God put us in the world to know, to love, and to serve him, and so come to paradise." (CCC, 1721)
>
> "The Beatitudes teach us the final end to which God calls us: the Kingdom, the vision of God, participation in the divine nature, eternal life, filiation, rest in God." (CCC, 1726)

This Beatitude, our ultimate happiness, lies not in the achievement of earthly success and the accumulation of riches. It lies, rather, in that very gift of salvation, won for us through the Cross of Christ.

> "How hard it is for those who have wealth to enter the kingdom of God. For it is easier for a camel to pass through the eye of a needle than for a rich person to enter the kingdom of God." Those who heard this said, "Then who can be saved?" And he said, "What is impossible for human beings is possible for God." (Lk 18:24-27)

Consider the analogy of the "thicket," as John of the Cross calls it in the above reference. That word conjures up in my mind the image of an adventure movie hero in search of the treasure of an ancient civilization. Machete in hand, he hacks his way through the dense undergrowth of the Amazon jungle in hopes of reaching the treasure held for centuries in some long-lost temple.

Applying this analogy to the spiritual realm, we want to remember, first of all, that Jesus Christ has already cleared miles of jungle growth, leaving but a few hundred yards of machete-hacking for us, to work our way through the thicket and reach the treasure. His "bulldozer" is the Cross, and our machete is the relatively little suffering to which each of us may be called. God has taken the initiative, loving us so much that he sent the Son to die to save us all. (Cf Jn 3:16) Our response, in turn, is to accept whatever hardships may be part of our homeward journey to the treasure of everlasting happiness.

> "Whoever wishes to come after me must deny himself, take up his cross, and follow me." (Mk 8:34)
>
> "I am the way and the truth and the life. No one comes to the Father except through me." (Jn 14:6)

Created for happiness, called to follow Christ, we will do well to gratefully accept our share of the Cross, knowing it is the narrow way that leads to life.

---

[1]The Liturgy of the Hours (New York: Catholic Book Publishing Co, 1975). Vol. I, 1246-7

15 God Is Good

It was September 24 of 2022, a full year following the accident. A thousand of us were gathered at the Delta by Marriott in Fargo for a Eucharistic Conference sponsored by the Diocese of Fargo as part of a three-year national program of Eucharistic Revival. We had been inspired by a quartet of keynote speakers from Friday evening through Saturday noon. The final afternoon session consisted of a service of healing prayer in the Eucharistic Presence of the Lord. For those unfamiliar with Exposition of the Blessed Sacrament, let me explain.

Bishop Folda placed a large host of the Holy Eucharist upon the altar in a vessel called the monstrance. Then we offered the traditional prayers and songs which accompany this action. But following that, the lay leader took us through a series of prayers designed to help open ourselves to whatever God may wish to do for us by way of physical, mental, emotional, and spiritual healing.

I have other physical concerns besides those related to the accident. A broken arm sustained during a high school wrestling incident left me with restricted mobility, reduced strength, and an arthritic wrist. Hearing loss, plaguing me for the past decade, is compensated for with the customary aid devices. In 1998 I submitted to LASIK surgery to correct severe nearsightedness.

Another minor nuisance resulting from the accident was my left eye, whose pupil would not properly contract in response to light. And of course, the weakened left knee and hip remained as reminders of my vulnerability.

The prayer leader suggested that to open ourselves to God's healing grace, we must search our hearts for anyone we might need to forgive, especially anyone who may have been responsible for our physical or emotional injury. The driver of the semi that rolled over my Alero came immediately to mind. So, I offered as much of a forgiveness prayer as I could muster at that moment.

Following the time of directed prayers, the leader invited anyone who had experienced some improvement of their condition to step forward and offer a testimony for the sake of encouraging us all to realize Jesus Christ is still active among us today. I could not at that moment notice any improvement in my own condition, so I refrained from going forward. But I sensed that I could still hope for God to help me in one of these relatively minor afflictions as time went on.

Fast forward now to some seventy-two hours later. I had joined the rest of our priests of the Fargo Diocese at our fall clergy education conference, held at the Gladstone Inn of Jamestown. We also went to the Basilica of Saint James for our periods of prayer and celebration of Mass. All the priests were to go forward to take Holy Communion at the altar. There was a nice ramp for the ascent to the altar, but the descent presented five intimidating steps. I thought of forcing my way back through the line of priests still ascending the ramp but opted to give the steps a try. "Lord, you've got to help me with this; I can't afford to fall," I breathed. Sure enough, with a modicum of grace-aided courage, I succeeded in negotiating the descent – planting my left foot on the first step at a forty-five degree angle, bending the knee and planting my right foot on the next, left foot on the third, right foot on the fourth, and reaching the last with the left, and a little celebratory fist pump discernible to my brother priests seated in the front row.

Encouraged by this minor victory, I decided to test myself on the walk back to the Gladstone Inn, half a mile away. Picking up the pace to what one might call a power walk, I strode with new determination. The effort went surprisingly well. I had never walked that fast for a year, and of course I had never run, careful not to overstress the weakened knee.

That was Monday evening. Earlier in the afternoon I had gone for my hundred minutes' walk, my newly established post-accident standard. On Tuesday I once again took our two-hour lunch break for the same hundred minutes' walk. But this time I chose to pick up the pace like I had done on the walk from the Basilica on Monday evening. The effort was surprisingly successful. In the same hundred minutes, I covered a good half-mile more than the previous day. Then as I negotiated the downhill descent toward the finish, I noticed something was missing -- my hip pain!

Let me clarify once more. Walking had already become relatively easy for my healthy heart and lungs, but still especially challenging for my left hip. Climbing and descending put extra strain on that muscle, reminding me I don't have the endurance my legs once enjoyed. But on Tuesday afternoon of September 27, I completed the walk without a hint of pain. Indeed, God is good. Call it coincidence, call it divine providence, call it the result of improved effort, call it what you will. I will give God credit for prompting me to step out and keep on trying.

It would be unrealistic, and inappropriate, to expect to be healed of every one of the tolerable limitations I suffer. Weakened eyes and ears and limbs are part of the lot of most every aging human being. Mortality is woven into the very fabric of our being. We are destined, after all, for life beyond this limited temporary existence. We look forward, as we pray in our Nicene Creed, to "the resurrection of the body to life everlasting." I, and every other person, must learn to live with limitations due to aging and illness and injury. My own afflictions simply place me in solidarity with all whose suffering is no doubt greater than mine. Our imperfect physical vessels will be replaced with new and perfect, glorified bodies, free of any of the weaknesses and afflictions we may have borne in this lifetime.

> "But we hold this treasure in earthen vessels, that the surpassing power may be of God and not from us. We are afflicted in every way, but not constrained; perplexed, but not driven to despair; persecuted, but not abandoned; struck down, but not destroyed; always carrying about in the body the dying of Jesus, so that the life of Jesus may also be manifested in our body. For we who live are constantly given up to death for the sake of Jesus, so that the life of Jesus may be manifested in our mortal flesh." (2 Cor 4:7-11)

> "Therefore, we are not discouraged; rather, although our outer self is wasting away, our inner self is being renewed day by day. For this momentary light affliction is producing for us an eternal weight of glory beyond all comparison, as we look not to what is seen but to what is unseen; for what is seen is transitory, but what is unseen is eternal." (2 Cor 4:16-18)

16 Gaining Through Loss

I am no stranger to loss of physical strength, agility, and endurance. Prior to my accident, the simple process of aging had already robbed me of a respectable running pace, though I was relatively happy to enjoy jogging at all. Just prior to those three-feet-from death injuries, my cardiovascular maintenance 10k consumed nearly eighty minutes at a 12-to-14-minutes per mile pace. "Accelerated ambling," I liked to call it, barely better than a fast-paced walk. The cumulative effect of four decades of dedicated running had taken its toll, primarily on my knee joints. Pain was a constant companion, though I had learned to live with it. If that pain and its effect on my running pace is considered a loss, then its tolerance was my gain.

In 2007, after foot surgeries correcting my bunion and hammertoe problems, I had already decided to run no more marathons. Rarely did my maintenance runs exceed six to eight miles after that. I ran the thirteen-mile half marathon in Fargo twice just to prove to myself I could still do it. But I knew it would be best to limit my training distances for the sheer sake of saving whatever knees I still had left. I was determined not to replace those aching natural knees with artificial ones if I could help it. You could say I was gaining common sense.

Come to think of it, I had experienced gain through loss much earlier in life. The year was 1964 and the day was Sunday, November 22. I remember it because it was exactly one year after the assassination of President John F. Kennedy. I was a high school junior at Cardinal Muench Seminary of Fargo. Father Leo Stelten, our Latin teacher, now deceased, had access to the Shanley High School gymnasium on Sunday afternoons, and was conducting a physical education program for the seminarians.

We were learning a few wrestling maneuvers. I was kneeling and bent forward with palms on the wrestling mat while my opponent held his arms around my chest. I was to work my way out of his hold. Nearly succeeding, I had twisted myself around clockwise and prepared to break free. At that moment I put my right arm out for leverage, and my opponent landed directly on that outstretched arm.

Everyone heard the crack of bones breaking . I had flipped back onto the mat in my starting position, with forearms resting on the mat, the front half of my fractured radius and ulna bent at a forty-five-degree angle from the rest of the limb. Father Stelten quickly supervised the process of stabilizing my arm and transporting me to the downtown hospital, then known as Saint Luke's. (It is currently known as the Sanford Broadway Medical Center.)

The doctor attending to my injury inserted an eight-inch-long rod through the elbow and fixed my arm in a plaster of Paris cast. I would live with the cast and sling for the next three months. My right arm would never be the same thereafter. I recall having three physical therapy sessions once the cast was removed and the rod was extracted. I will never forget the momentary but intense pain of that extraction. The therapist did his best to work with me on exercises to improve my capacity to rotate and straighten the forearm. To this day, when I lay my upper arm and elbow flat on a table with palm facing upward, I cannot make the forearm touch; the back of my hand is fully four inches above the table surface. Arthritis limits the flexibility of my right wrist, and its pain is a constant reminder of the injury. For any task requiring strength, I favor the use of my left hand and arm.

The day before that wrestling injury, I had proudly done eighty pushups, part of my daily exercise routine. I have never done more than twenty-five or thirty ever since, and I use the compromised right arm as a handy excuse for poor golf scores. But that whole experience taught me to live with the situation of loss and rise above it.

After my brief hospitalization for that wrestling injury, I resumed my regular class schedule. My left arm and hand became my friend. Writing was the most difficult skill to master, but I managed to scrawl the necessary notes in Sister Rosaria's chemistry class, to pass the exams and maintain my A-studded report card. Father Arth, the seminary rector, included an A-plus for effort that quarter. And once my right arm emerged from the cast, I was well on my way to ambidexterity. I would continue to use my left hand for many of the tasks it had performed by necessity, awkwardly at first and more gracefully as the weeks wore on.

I still employ alternate hands for eating, for cleaning the sacred vessels at the altar, and various other tasks. Gaining relative ambidexterity was another source of pride, another testimony to my spirit of determination. I would never let misfortune get me down. Two years after taking up the game of golf at age fifty-five, I decided to purchase a set of left-handed clubs. Thinking my stronger left arm might help me hit the ball farther or straighter, I was pleasantly surprised to discover I was equally capable --and mediocre --from the get-go. I did resume right-handed golfing after two years of that experiment.

After having nearly lost my life, I could once again count my blessings, having the simple ability to walk the golf course in the spring of 2022, and swing a club, and gleefully report in my Christmas letter that December, "I am golfing as poorly as ever."

Following my car accident and the slow but steady recovery process, I realized that it would be wise not to start running again even if I could. Why should I risk re-injuring my knees at this age? I also decided to surrender my plan of hiking the entire Appalachian Trail upon retirement. Being able to walk was gain enough for me after the damage to my legs on the day I could easily have lost my life. I considered every bit of progress a cause for gratitude. Happily, choosing to walk instead of run, I gained the prize of pain-free knees, a luxury I had not enjoyed for many years. Before the accident, I could not sit in the confined space of an airplane seat without serious discomfort by mid-flight. In every physical loss, I have found a gain to celebrate.

Much more important than these physical gains and losses, is the spiritual reward one can reap amid challenging situations. While lying in my hospital bed at Sanford on September 15, 2021, I thanked God for his merciful gift of a second chance on life. Pondering my past use of time and talents and energies, I considered what I might do better from that point on.

The first and most obvious thing was to enhance the frequency and quality of my prayer. Admittedly, I had been lax in observing the daily recitation of the prayer known as the Divine Office or Liturgy of Hours. When we are ordained as deacons, the first level of Holy Orders, we promise to pray this "Divine Office" faithfully each day. To default on this promise, then, is considered a sinful neglect. So, I decided this pattern of laxity would change immediately. I can happily report that from that day forward until the day of this writing, I have prayed every segment of every day's prayers: the Office of Readings, Morning, Daytime, Evening, and Nighttime Prayer. On especially busy and demanding days, I may offer some of these at a later period of the day, but the prayer is done. Previously, I might have missed an entire day of those prayers without giving it a second thought. Knowing the need to keep my priorities in better balance, physical fitness now began to take second place to spiritual wellness.

I am well aware of the need to spend more time in prayer, and to seek a better quality of prayer in addition to its quantity. The "holy hour" spent before the Blessed Sacrament is the gold standard for the priest who is serious about living his call to the fullest and growing ever closer to Christ personally and in his ministry. I cannot yet lay claim to achievement of that standard, but you will find me in prayer before the Blessed Sacrament much more frequently than ever before. This, too, is a gain to celebrate.

This balancing of priorities should have happened much earlier, but my serious wakeup call became the occasion for me to renew my commitment to the discipline of the Liturgy of Hours. I gained the resolve to make every effort to act on the daily graces God gives, to conduct myself in a way pleasing to God. The urgency of preparing for eternal life came to me loud and clear. This should be the goal of every person of faith. "The most important thing to do in this life is to be ready for the next." This became a new mantra for the renewed self I gleefully call "Father Dale 2.0"

Suffice it to say that I am learning as I go, and the Office of Readings will often hit home for me in my post-accident condition in a way they may not have before I experienced this near loss of life.

Take for example this reading from one of the Catecheses by Saint Cyril of Jerusalem (Cat 13:1.3.6.23)

> "Paul says 'God forbid that I should glory in anything but the cross of our Lord Jesus Christ!' At Siloam, there was a sense of

> wonder, and rightly so. A man born blind recovered his sight. But of what importance is this, when there are so many blind people in the world? Lazarus rose up from the dead, but even this affected only Lazarus. What of those countless numbers who have died because of their sins? Those five miraculous loaves fed five thousand people. Yet this is a small number compared to those all over the world who were starved by ignorance."
>
> "For us all, however, the Cross is the crown of victory! It has brought light to those blinded by ignorance. It has released those enslaved by sin Indeed, it has redeemed the whole of humankind!"

From this reading I gleaned the awareness that while I was spared from physical death through a miraculous intervention, there are so many others less fortunate. Traffic fatalities occur by the thousands across our nation annually. I am, in a sense, the lucky Lazarus who won the lottery whose prize is a few more years on earth. What of all those others who died, and the families who grieve their loss? Why no miracle for them?

While ruminating on that question, I realized the greater concern beyond my amazing physical rescue is the salvation of my soul. The cross of suffering I bore through the experience of the accident has served as an instrument of my redemption. Similarly, those who bear the cross of losing a loved one may find consolation in knowing Christ died for the eternal salvation of those beloved who have already gone on before us.

Jesus gave us an important teaching about gaining spiritually through loss:

> "Whoever wishes to come after me must deny himself, take up his cross, and follow me. For whoever wishes to save his life will

> lose it, but whoever loses his life for my sake and that of the gospel will save it. What profit is there for one to gain the whole world and forfeit his life? What could one give in exchange for his life?" (Mk 8:34-37)

By wishing to "save one's own life," Jesus means our self-possession, and the stuff of earthly life to which we too readily cling. For me, that would be the athletic prowess of my cardiovascular fitness pursuits. Good as the effort to preserve one's physical well-being is per se, it does not get one to heaven. One must become spiritually fit by "losing one's life for the sake of Christ and the gospel." In self-surrender, we let go of our desire for fame and fortune in favor of growing rich in the sight of God, serving the divine will for our salvation. What we lose in giving up our pursuit of earthly pleasure is relatively minor in comparison to the great gain of the lasting treasure of grace.

Losses of the earthly kind may well loom large for us while we suffer them. This is part of the fabric of fallen human nature. Adam and Eve, upon their expulsion from the garden of Eden, heard the Lord God tell them,

> "I will intensify the pangs of your childbearing; in pain shall you bring forth children . . . by the sweat of your face shall you get bread to eat, until you return to the ground, from which you were taken; for you are dirt, and unto dirt you shall return." (Gen 3:16,19)

Earthly life is fraught with challenges, with disappointments, with losses, with illness, and finally with death, the ultimate physical loss. Yet the very sin of Adam and Eve that ushered in this life of loss, would become the occasion for God to work wondrously, generously, mercifully to help us regain the very kind of happiness for which we were originally created.

As we sing in the Easter Proclamation known as the Exultet:

> "To ransom a slave, you gave away your Son! O truly necessary sin of Adam, destroyed completely by the death of Christ. O happy fault that earned so great, so glorious a Redeemer."[1]

And as Paul writes in his letter to the Philippians, reflecting on his former life and his newfound life in Christ:

> "Whatever gains I had, I have come to consider a loss because of Christ. More than that, I even consider everything as a loss because of the supreme good of knowing Christ Jesus my Lord. For his sake I have accepted the loss of all things and I consider them so much rubbish, that I may gain Christ and be found in him, not having any righteousness of my own based on the law but that which comes through faith in Christ, the righteousness from God, depending on faith to know him and the power of his resurrection and the sharing of his sufferings by being conformed to his death, if somehow I may attain the resurrection from the dead." (Phil 3:7-11)

Paul's reference to considering the loss of things as "so much rubbish" brings to mind the analogy of a pair of binoculars with a different lens in each of its two eyepieces. There are two contrasting lenses, two contrasting ways of viewing earthly realities. If we look at things such as popularity, possessions, and physical prowess through the "left eye," the lens of self-concern, they seem so large, so important. On the other hand, viewing them through the "right eye," the lens of faith, they seem so much smaller relative to the things of eternal worth. With that lens of faith held up to the eyes of heart and soul, we can focus more clearly on the distant shore, the heavenly destination of our journey.

Through the lens of faith, we can look beyond the labor pains of the moment and the bread earned by the sweat of our brow, seeing in them our share of the cross of Christ, losing ourselves for him and for the sake of the gospel. Being more closely conformed to the death of Christ, we may truly attain our resurrection from the dead with him.

Examining my own narrow escape from physical death on the Feast of the Holy Cross through the lens of faith, the message came clear to me. Christ was mercifully inviting me, once again, to deny myself, to take up my cross and follow him, to lose my life for his sake and that of the gospel, and in so doing to save it.

How small the loss, and how great the gain.

---

[1]*The Roman Missal*, English Translation According to the Third Typical Edition, Liturgy of the Easter Vigil

17 Hidden Blessings

One of the obvious hidden blessings in this whole experience of the serious car accident was the immediate cessation of my spending on the gas I would have burned driving to all the activities in which I would have otherwise engaged. While I lay in the hospital bed and convalesced in the PAM Rehabilitation facility, I was not spending any money on personal pursuits. Mind you, I would much rather have been healthy and accident-free, so that I could have gone on with life as usual. But the sudden interruption of the lifestyle I took so much for granted forced me to take a good long look at the way I was doing things, including my driving habits.

I decided I would need to treat the newer vehicle waiting at home in my garage much kinder. That was the 2016 Chevy Trax I had acquired in 2018 with 15,000 miles on the odometer. I had already driven another 55,000 miles in that car besides the miles driven in the Alero. Over the span of three years, then, the combined total of my travels with the two vehicles was 150,000 miles! Half of that was business travel, non-negotiable. But the other half was personal miles, including all the trips to area golf courses, shopping trips to Fargo, long distance trips to visit family and friends, and so on. One could argue that each of these personal trips were justifiable in and of themselves. Yet the overall picture of excessive driving was a subject I have now taken time to reconsider. You can bet that I will rein in the number of unnecessary trips, while still giving myself permission to do such personally uplifting things in moderation.

Another hidden blessing, and this I believe is God's sense of humor, was the opportunity to address my retirement dilemma. I have shared my well-laid-out plan to hike the Appalachian Trail upon retirement. I wanted to do that right away for a couple reasons. First, I had never in all my years of priesthood taken what we call a sabbatical, a period away from our regular parish assignments for study or enrichment. Believing I would certainly deserve a time of several months undisturbed, to "do my own thing," I figured this would be the right time.

Those of us priests who retire, and are still healthy enough for normal activity, are soon in demand to serve as weekend substitutes. Other priests in active parish assignments want us retirees to cover their weekend Masses so they can go on vacation or retreats and the like. I was going to hike from July through November. Then I would come back and be available, knowing I would most likely be in great demand the moment I finished the Appalachian endeavor.

Second, I would be suffering the anxiety of moving from my current rectory into whatever apartment dwelling I would have to secure. I had not yet determined where that might be. But in any case, all the logistics of downsizing to move into a much smaller space loomed large in my mind. How would I move out at the end of June in 2024, my 75th year of life and 50th year of priesthood, and settle in a new place quickly enough to hit the Appalachian Trail by the Fourth of July? And what about the November weather, which could get nasty even in Georgia, the southern terminus of the trail?

I had already thought of renting a U-Haul truck a month earlier and moving my vastly reduced inventory to the location I would no doubt have chosen by then. Would I have to pay five months' rent down to secure the place until my return from the long trek? Or could I be "homeless" for those months and bank whatever pension I was not spending on the hiking project? What about paying the inevitable bills, getting mail, renewing medical prescriptions, and so on? Would I be able to do all the necessary business through my smart phone?

As you see, my entire plan presented a double challenge. Doing the long hike would be challenging enough, without all the other concerns involved in moving. So, God's sense of humor, as I see it, was to remove one of the two sources of anxiety. I can just hear Jesus saying, with a smile, "Thanks to this accident, you will only have one thing to worry about at a time!"

Another hidden blessing was the forced reassessment of my daily routine. Naturally, I had been doing the parish ministry and office work one would expect of an active pastor. But I justified plenty of free time for television, solitaire games on the smart phone and any number of side interests. While lying in thc hospital bed and sitting in my wheelchair for the long hours and days of rehabilitation, I decided my first priority should be prayer. While I was healthy and well, I had become sloppy about that aspect of life.

Now, realizing God gave me this second chance on life, it came to me loud and clear, that prayer will be the non-negotiable priority from this day forward. God has given me this extra time on earth, after all. God, who knows our inmost thoughts, knows I am determined He will receive his daily due from this priest grateful for one more day on earth.

> "But when you pray, go to your inner room, close your door, and pray to your Father in secret. And your Father who sees in secret will repay you." (Mt 6:6)

18 Home Field Advantage

> "Yes, we do have confidence, and we would rather be away from the body and at home with the Lord. So, whether we are at home or away, we make it our aim to be pleasing to him. For all of us must appear before the judgment seat of Christ, so that each may receive due recompense for actions done in the body, whether good or evil." (2 Cor 5:8-10, NRSV)

Paul writes a most fitting description of our spiritual dilemma: life on this earth among family and friends is a great blessing, yet our final destiny is everlasting union with God in heaven. That destiny -- eternal reward or punishment -- will ultimately depend on God's judgment of our "actions done in the body, whether good or evil."

While lying in my hospital bed the very day after my accident of September 14, I reflected on that split second when, seeing myself and my Alero sliding under the semi-truck trailer, my soul silently screamed, "Lord, I'm not ready yet!" Pondering the state of my soul, I resolved then and there to do my best to do nothing that would displease the Lord. I committed myself to "make it my aim to be pleasing to him." My new mantra going forward from that day became, "The most important thing for me to do in this life is to be ready for the next."

"Whether at home or away, we make it our aim to be pleasing to him." That verse made me think of the various sports contests in which we take interest. I enjoy going to our local football and basketball games, and I am a diehard Minnesota Twins and Vikings fan, loyally supporting my nearest professional teams, as well as the North Dakota State University Bison on the college level.

Whatever the contest, the spectators cheering for their home team supply that extra energy and incentive we call home field advantage. Sometimes the "twelfth player on the team," the crowd of spectators, shouts so loudly the opposing quarterback is hard pressed to communicate signals to his fellow players. Home field advantage may also consist of the positive vibrations from playing in the presence of our cheering fans.

Let us apply this analogy of the home field advantage in sports to the spiritual contest in which we are all actively engaged -- the quest for eternal happiness in heaven. This is our ultimate contest, in which victory over the forces of evil is vital. Our spiritual opponents, Satan and his minions, are fixed on bringing us down in defeat. Our team captain, Jesus Christ, has in fact already won the victory over those forces of evil through his cross and resurrection. But we must each enter the playing field and take our role on the team, doing our best to seal the victory and claim it as our own.

"The earth is the Lord's and everything in it, the world and all who live in it." (Ps 24:1) We are playing on the home field; our spiritual adversary is the away team. Yet Satan has the skills to deceive us, to divert us from our goal, if we let our guard down. God will always give us grace sufficient to thwart those deceptive tactics we call temptations.

In the Office of Readings from the Liturgy of Hours for December 24, we hear from a sermon by Bishop Saint Augustine of Hippo:

"You would have suffered eternal death, had he not been born in time. Never would you have been freed from sinful flesh, had he not taken upon himself the likeness of sinful flesh. You would have suffered everlasting unhappiness, had it not been for this mercy. You would never have returned to life, had he not shared your death. You would have been lost if he had not hastened to your aid. You would have perished, had he not come. Let us then joyfully celebrate the coming of our salvation and redemption. Let us celebrate the festive day on which he who is the great and eternal day came from the great and endless day of eternity into our own short day of time."[1]

Jesus Christ came onto the field as our player coach, entering the contest on our behalf. He became one with all the players who ever lived, past and present and future. He turned the seeming defeat of sin and death into the victory of everlasting life with the saints of heaven. He gives us home field advantage.

---

[1]Sermo 185, PL 38, 997-999, in Liturgy of Hours Vol. 1, 379-80

19 Fears and Favors

"Oh Lord, is this how I'm going to die? I'm not ready yet!" Fear of death consumed me on September 14, 2021, at the very moment of my crash. Only a day later, racked with pain but grateful to be alive, I pondered the divine favor of another chance on life. Friends who reached out to me reaffirmed my awareness of the special favor of my narrow escape from death. That day was the Feast of the Triumph of the Holy Cross, and the connection of my own injuries to Christ's suffering for the sake of our salvation was indelibly fixed in my mind.

Fifteen months later, on the 8th of December in 2022, those two words, fear and favor, leapt out at me while reflecting on the Scriptures of yet another great feast in our church calendar. For Catholic Christians, that is the day we celebrate the Solemnity of the Immaculate Conception of the Blessed Virgin Mary. According to our firmly held teaching, God favored her with the exceptional privilege of being spared from the stain of original sin, the negative effects of the sin of Adam and Eve. God would grant her this favor to prepare in her a worthy dwelling for Jesus, the Son of God, who would spend his first nine months in her womb. (Cf. CCC 490-493)

The Gospel reading chosen for that feast day presents the moment of the Annunciation, in which Angel Gabriel greets Mary, "Hail, full of grace, the Lord is with you." And as she troubles over these words, Gabriel continues, "Do not be afraid, Mary, for you have found favor with God. And behold, you shall conceive in your womb and bear a son, and you shall call his name Jesus." (Cf. Lk 1:26-32)

Gabriel explains this miracle of a virgin birth is to be empowered by the Holy Spirit, "for with God, nothing will be impossible." Mary then grace-fully responds, "Behold, I am the handmaid of the Lord; let it be done to me according to your word." (Cf. Lk 1:37-38)

Contrasting Mary's "Yes" to God at that moment, we read the Genesis passage where Adam and Eve, responding with their "No" to God's command, sinfully partake of the forbidden fruit, then hide themselves from the presence of the Lord, who comes in search of them in the garden. Adam responds to God, "I was afraid because I was naked, and I hid myself." And Eve responds, "The serpent beguiled me, and I ate." (Cf. Gen 3:8-13)

So, our original parents scurried away from God in fear, in guilt and shame over their sin. That is what we do, in effect, each time we sin personally. God would have us remain near him in words and deeds of grace, yet we scurry away in the opposite direction, defying the divine will in favor of doing our own thing. We hide ourselves spiritually, fearful of facing the fact our misdeeds merit the punishment of expulsion from the Heavenly Garden of Paradise. Like little children, we hide away in our little cubby hole, thinking mom and dad may not know where to find us, when in fact they know exactly where we are, and probably know what we have just done that caused us to run to our favorite place of refuge. Fear of punishment leaves us at a physical and emotional distance from our loving parents.

Catholics familiar with the prayer called the Act of Contrition, recited in preparation to receive absolution in the Sacrament of Reconciliation, may recall the words of the older traditional formula: "Oh my God, I am heartily sorry for having offended thee, because I dread the loss of heaven and the pains of hell, but most of all because they offend thee, my God, who are all good and deserving of all my love."

Christians universally recognize the sevenfold Gifts of the Holy Spirit, gifts strengthened by grace when we receive Confirmation. Among these gifts is one called Fear of the Lord. (CCC 1831, cf. Is 11:1-2) This gift is essentially what we mean by saying we "dread the loss of heaven and the pains of hell." We dread the thought of eternal separation from the Father who loves us so much he sacrificed his Son on the Cross to open the gates of Paradise for us once more. It is a positive fear, inducing us to hasten toward our merciful Lord for the forgiveness he so readily grants, so we no longer need hide behind the fig leaves of our shame.

Fears of the negative kind shackle us in the prison of limited existence. I had to overcome my serious fear of the water to successfully complete the 2.4-mile swim leg of my Ironman Triathlon. As a boy, fear of being ridiculed for my knobby knees kept me from taking swimming lessons when our Lisbon pool offered them over the summer. It was not until age twenty-four that I attempted my first swim of over a hundred yards.

Fear of separation from home for a week of camp, and fear of poor performance in outdoor activities, kept me from joining Boy Scouts when my friend urged me to join along with him. Those were fears I had to overcome by facing them later in life. I still face my fear of heights each time I climb a ladder to clean autumn leaves out of the rain gutters. Okay, I know there are gutter guards, but the ones I installed haven't fully eliminated the need to climb up there to do annual maintenance anyway.

Then there is a positive kind of fear we might better call respect. A healthy fear of collision causes us to slow down when road conditions are less than ideal. Those of us who endure winters in the Upper Midwest know exactly what I am talking about. We respect the driving laws and the rules of common sense, caring for our own well-being.

A healthy respect of the bison herd resting smack dab in the middle of a wide-open flat plateau section of the hiking trail in Theodore Roosevelt National Park in the North Dakota Badlands led me to carefully work my way around them on the downwind side of the trail, and to resist taking a picture lest I spook them with the glint of my camera lens facing into the rising sun. Had they arisen and headed toward me at that moment, there would have been no place of refuge. I had to respect those creatures possessing a size and strength and speed superior to my own.

The gift of Fear of the Lord, then, is born of the positive kind of respect we have for the commands God has given us as guideposts leading us heavenward on our earthly hike. Fearing calamitous misstep, we tread the Way of the will of God for humankind, desiring to stay safe within the realm of divine grace. The pain of loss we feel at separation from our loved ones who precede us in death pales to insignificance in comparison to the eternal pain of separation from God and neighbor in hell if that should be our final destiny. Let us fear that separation so deeply that we hasten to our merciful God in repentance and sorrow for the sins by which we hid in guilt and shame.

One of the positive outcomes of my accident, then, was a rekindled fear of the Lord, stirring my resolve to do nothing so serious as to separate myself from God's redeeming grace. I renewed my resolve to open myself to serve the divine will for my life as fully as possible. With Mary I want to respond, "I am the servant of the Lord, let it be done to me according to your word."

Enough on fears. Let's focus now on favors. The Epistle reading for our Mass of the Immaculate Conception was taken from the first chapter of Paul's letter to the Ephesians. The verse that caught my attention reads: "In love he destined us for adoption to himself through Jesus Christ, in accord with the favor of his will, for the praise of the glory of his grace that he granted us in the beloved," (Eph 1:5-6, NAB)

Other translations render verse 5 "according to the purpose of his will" (RSV) or "the pleasure of his will." (NRSV). But verse 6 proved to be of greatest interest, and the translations align more closely: "for the praise of the glory of his grace" (NAB); "to the praise of his glorious grace" (RSV); "to the praise of the glory of his grace" (NRSV). The term for this grace in Greek, in which the letter was written, is *charis*. This Greek word, in fact, is the same one we find in Luke 1:30, "for you have found favor with God." (NAB, RSV, NRSV)

As a result of this bit of research, my anxiety over the word favor was nicely resolved. The divine favor of which we are speaking is truly a gift of God's grace freely given, not due to any merit of ours. My rescue and my second chance in life was clearly a charis. I wager that God had already chosen to grant this favor regardless of the celestial conference of which I wrote earlier. But I submit that God wants to involve the heavenly choir of angels and saints in their role of interceding for us. They are, after all, the cloud of witnesses who cheer us on in running the race to the finish line of the marathon that matters, to join them in claiming the prize of eternal happiness.

Just a bit further on in his letter to the Ephesians, Paul writes,

> "For by *grace* you have been saved through faith, and this is not your own doing; it is the gift of God – not the result of works, so that you may boast. For we are what he has made us, created in Christ Jesus for good works, which God prepared beforehand to be our way of life." (Eph 2:8-10, NRSV)

These words remind us we are spiritually saved from the clutches of sin by grace, the gift of God given in Christ. Faith, itself a gift of God, brings us to recognize and accept the gift of our salvation. Then consider each day another *charis*, another free gift of our loving God, enabling us to do whichever of those *good works God has prepared for us beforehand.*

Let us not be anxious whether we are picking the activities God has in mind for us on any given day. Let us, rather, examine our lifestyle and consider whether our behaviors are true to the way in which God would have us walk. Thoughts, words, and actions contrary to a godly way of life must cease. Those which properly serve the will of God, letting it "be done to us according to his word," will then naturally emerge as the demands of the day present themselves.

"God has kept you alive for a reason; your work is not finished yet." Such affirming words from many friends and community members remind me God has prepared beforehand any number of good works I may still do in whatever time remains for me on earth. I have wondered at times whether that means I should become a missionary in a distant land or serve the poorest of the poor in the streets of Calcutta like Saint Mother Teresa. But such noble vocations do not seem to be the ones for which I was gifted. I will seek guidance and prayerfully discern the best way of placing myself at the Lord's service, and rest in confident assurance I am doing whatever I can to "become the best version of myself," as author Matthew Kelly describes it.[1] I encourage every reader to do the same.

My new mantra is, **"The most important thing for me in this life is to make sure I am ready for the next."** But it would be foolishly selfish of me to think all that remains is to make sure I get to heaven. There is good work yet to be done, people yet to be served. When I awake in the morning, I want to ask God **"What would you have me do to honor and serve you today?"** And generally, there is enough to do right in the streets of my own community, that I can't even worry about ministering among the poor of Calcutta. I pray God will raise up others who will respond to that special call, to the favor of God's grace inspiring them to say yes to that much needed ministry to the poor and the oppressed throughout the world.

Reflecting more intently on the words we Christians all pray so regularly, the Lord's Prayer, I reminded myself we ask, "THY kingdom come, THY will be done," not "MY will be done."

Overcoming our fears of the enslaving kind, the kind that would have us scurry away and hide from God, let us forge ahead with fear of the Lord, acting on the favor of God's grace to accomplish the good work God has in mind for us. Let us not be afraid, for we too have found favor with God.

---

[1]Matthew Kelly, *Becoming the Best Version of Yourself*, available on CD through www.dynamiccatholic.com, SKU#BBVY-09-CD-ENG

See also Kelly, *Perfectly Yourself: Discovering God's Dream for You* (North Palm Beach, FL: Beacon Publishing, 3rd ed., 2017)

20 Worthy Work

"Your work on earth must not be done yet." "God still has more work for you to do." Remarks of this sort were very common in conversations about my accident. I readily agreed with anyone making this observation, acknowledging the hand of providence at work in my rescue.

It is amazing to think of all the talents, energies and resources employed on my behalf from September 14, 2021, the day of my accident, through early April of 2022 when my rehabilitation therapy was completed.

"To Protect and Serve," the motto of our police forces, may well apply to many of the helping professions. I am grateful for the patrolman who helped control traffic while the Cooperstown Fire and Rescue volunteers freed me from my crushed Alero. Those men, and the nurse at my side, gave of their time and talents to save a life.

The farmer who came to my side and called 911 immediately is to be commended for his quick response and good thinking. As a matter of fact, the whole farming profession is a challenging one, and we should all be grateful for the long hours, the huge financial outlay, and the energies they invest from planting to harvest time and throughout the year. Theirs is an accident-prone occupation. Over the years, I have responded to several emergency calls requiring the presence of a priest for anointing of a seriously injured farmer. Theirs is a truly noble and sacrificial work. Thanks to their dedication, the world is fed.

I must add truck drivers here too, because, although my encounter of September 14 was not a happy one, we must realize the risks they all take when climbing into their rigs to deliver products to market across our land, including the agricultural chemicals our farmers need.

Think, then, of all the medical personnel and resources employed in the air flight, the surgeries and hospitalization at Fargo Sanford -- the doctors, nurses and aides, x-ray technicians and anesthetists, patient caseworkers, insurance claim representatives, and supplemental staff needed to attend to my care. Then there were the priests ready at hand to offer the sacrament of anointing prior to each of my surgeries – the immediate surgical repair of the fractured right leg and the left knee repair a week later.

My transfer to PAM Rehabilitation Hospital would employ another host of talented professionals. The therapists, the consulting doctor, the aides, the desk staff who delivered my mail, the nutrition team, the custodians who cleaned the room, all played a role in my personal well-being and recovery.

Upon my release to home health care and occupational therapy in Cooperstown, I received quality personal attention. Meals on Wheels came faithfully each weekday, and South-Central Transit took me to follow-up appointments in Fargo. By early November I would begin outpatient therapy with the skilled team at Cooperstown Medical Center.

While never wishing this accident upon myself, I offered prayers of thanks for all who played a role in my treatment and recovery throughout those many months. I have no doubt forgotten to acknowledge many other professionals whose work underlies the services from which I benefited. Experiencing the work of those I have named gives me new appreciation of everything these professions do to protect and serve the physical, mental, and spiritual well-being of all who need their care. Theirs is worthy work, indeed.

Among the references cited in the Catechism of the Catholic Church regarding work is that of Pope John Paul II, *Laborem Exercens*, a thorough treatment on the dignity of human work, promulgated on September 14, 1981, the Feast of the Holy Cross.[1] Ironically, by providential happenstance, my accident would occur exactly on the fortieth anniversary of the document's promulgation. There, in Section V on "Elements for a Spirituality of Work," we read:

> "The word of God's revelation is profoundly marked by the fundamental truth that man, created in the image of God, shares by his work in the activity of the Creator and that, within the limits of his own capabilities, man in a sense continues to develop that activity, and perfects it as he advances further in the discovery of the resources and values contained in the whole of creation. We find this truth at the very beginning of Sacred Scripture, in the Book of Genesis, where the creation activity in itself is presented in the form of 'work' done by God during 'six days,' 'resting' on the seventh day. Besides, the last book of Sacred Scripture echoes the same respect for what God has done through his creative 'work' when it proclaims: 'Great and wonderful are your deeds, O Lord God the Almighty'; this is similar to the Book of Genesis, which concludes the description of each day of creation with the statement: 'And God saw that it was good.'" (LE, 25)

Our individual work is one expression of our human dignity. Formed in the image of our Creator, we are divinely commissioned to protect the earth and its creatures, and to serve the common good of mankind.

Further, as the Catholic Catechism notes:

> "Work honors the Creator's gifts and the talents received from him. It can also be redemptive. By enduring the hardship of work in union with Jesus, the carpenter of Nazareth and the one crucified on Calvary, man collaborates in a certain fashion with the Son of God in his redemptive work. He shows himself to be a disciple of Christ by carrying the cross, daily, in the work he is called to accomplish. Work can be a means of sanctification and a way of animating earthly realities with the Spirit of Christ." (CCC, 2427)

So, the worthy work done on my behalf is but one example of the discipleship of Christ in action whenever we take up the cross of serving one another. Considering our work as a way of uniting us with Christ who bore the Cross for us in his most important work of redemption, gives me one more clue to the reason God allowed my accident to occur on the Feast of the Holy Cross.

> "The Christian finds in human work a small part of the Cross of Christ and accepts it in the same spirit of redemption in which Christ accepted his Cross for us. In work, thanks to the light that penetrates us from the Resurrection of Christ, we always find a glimmer of new life, of the new good, as if it were an announcement of 'the new heavens and the new earth' in which man and the world participate precisely though the toil that goes with work." (LE, 27)

Although I will move on into retirement shortly after composing this work, I still anticipate some "productive toil" in the years ahead. I will continue to exercise priestly ministry in some form, substituting where needed, without the administrative responsibilities of a parish pastor. Being a priest who has helped present the talks on Marriage Encounter weekends since 1979, I fully intend to continue availing myself to those weekends as well. "My work is not done, and God has something more for me to do."

> "If I go on living in the flesh, that means fruitful labor for me." (Eph 1:22)

God's work continues to this very day through each person's response to a God-given vocational call. Our sacrificial work is one facet of the precious jewel, the "pearl of great price," (cf. Mt 13:46) purchased by Christ in the Triumph of the Holy Cross.

---

[1]His Holiness, John Paul II, Encyclical, Laborem Exercens, (September 14, 1981)

21 Pernicious Presumption

Being physically fit as I was, I had presumed I would live to at least age 96 or so, just as my father had done, or even to 94 like my mother. Dad was a smoker and had COPD (chronic obstructive pulmonary disease) later in life, though he quit smoking at age 62 under doctor's orders. That act of obedience no doubt lengthened his life considerably.

I, on the other hand, had never smoked more than the single puff dad let me take from one of his lighted cigarettes as a curious four-year-old. So, when medical practitioners ask that question about tobacco use, I love to joke, "I quit when I was four." As a non-smoker and an avid runner and cardiovascular fitness buff, I figured I would be one of those most likely to make it to a hundred, barring cancer or some other major catastrophe such as a car accident. "I am running now because I want to be able to walk when I am ninety," I would quip, seeking to justify my athletic endeavors.

Let the reader understand that I am a strong advocate of physical exercise to enhance the quality of life for every American. I shudder when I see so many struggling with obesity and the related problems of heart disease and diabetes. We are needlessly shortening our life spans by lack of attention to basic principles of nutrition and healthy lifestyle. These things are readily within our control if we exercise the willpower to improve our habits of diet and exercise.

Beyond that, however, are many factors beyond our control. Genetics play a role in family longevity, as we know. Cancer and other invasive diseases take their toll on young lives all too often. I have been so fortunate, thus far, to escape major medical issues. But on September 14 of 2021, all my presumptions were instantly dashed to pieces.

I call my presumption "pernicious" because I had assumed an admittedly arrogant stance, that I would remain one of the healthiest members of my age group right on through my eighties and nineties. Even as I lay in the crushed Alero, gasping for breath and waiting in pain as the rescue squad worked to extricate me and get me to the helicopter, I realized I could easily have died that day.

Then as I lay in my hospital bed the day following my first surgery, I realized further that pernicious presumption had lulled me into a sense of complacency about the state of my soul. Certainly, I was doing the basic things expected of my role as a priest and pastor of the flock under my care. But I was neglecting the well-being of my own spiritual life. By analogy, my soul had grown obese through lack of disciplined exercise. I will note, however, that the daily celebration of Holy Mass, with the reading of Sacred Scripture, the consecration and reception of Holy Eucharist, is the "source and summit" of my spiritual life.[1] So, essentially, I was in decent shape, spiritually speaking.

When Bishop Folda came to visit me at the PAM Rehabilitation Hospital that first weekend, I admitted I had grown lax in my practice of praying the Liturgy of Hours, or Divine Office as it is known. From that day forward, I would not miss a single unit of the five periods of daily prayer the Liturgy of Hours entails. My ideal, of course, is to offer the Readings and Morning Prayer the very first thing upon rising, and then observe Daytime Prayer, Evening Prayer, and Night Prayer at appropriate times. Sometimes the demands of the day may delay my use of the Office of Readings and Morning Prayer, but I would always make room for them at some point later in the day. Why do Morning Prayer at noon if I missed it earlier? I value its merit, reflecting on the Psalms and Scripture readings it offers, at whatever time of the day I open the book or go to the iBreviary smartphone app to pray.

Every one of us needs to work at finding some sweet spot of "down time" we can fill with prayer and meditation. Here again, I sometimes find myself offering Evening and Night Prayer at the end of the day before retiring. But there is always time, each day without fail. One must make the time, by making it a priority. I knew this was one of the reasons for which God spared me from death that day, so that I could take my prayer discipline more seriously and restore the balance of bodily and spiritual health in my own life. Additional forms of prayer such as meditating on the Scriptures and spending a holy hour before the Blessed Sacrament will enrich my life, and the life of any person who engages in them.

Pernicious presumption led me to a habit of procrastination on so many things that should be done sooner rather than later. I operate by meeting deadlines, finishing tasks no sooner than necessary. My modus operandi has been to avoid spending too long at the things I rather not do. I simply save them until last and let the stress be intense but bearably brief, as I rush to complete the task at hand. Those of you who have learned to work on your assigned projects early and finish them on time may shake your heads at my way of being and doing.

I would love to change my style, frankly, but I have gotten away with it for so long, it is hard to change. Pernicious presumption, that I will finish by the time the project is due, persists post-accident. I have not yet experienced the same sense of urgency about getting the affairs of my office in order, as I have the affairs of my soul. Life would be easier if I would make punctuality and good order a higher priority. This, then, is my personal "lifestyle obesity," with which I will probably struggle for the rest of my days. Life would be easier if I would simply shed those extra pounds of procrastination and clutter, but my perniciously ingrained habit has prevailed to the day of this writing.

In sum, there are things we can readily change by exercise of willpower, and other things we probably will not master, due to the collective weakening of will that we may blame on Adam and Eve. Pernicious presumption led them to listen to the Serpent's claim that eating of the fruit of the Tree of Knowledge of Good and Evil would not harm them, contrary to the divine warning, "You shall not eat of it nor even touch it, lest you die." (Cf. Gen 3:1-7) We label their sin one of pride, wherein they placed their own perceived benefit above the divinely given knowledge of good and evil.

Each of our personal sins is basically a revisiting of that same prideful presumption, "We know better than God at this moment." Despite knowing internally by conscience what is best for our long-term well-being, we often choose that which serves a more appealing short-term goal. In my own example, I would rather relax at the television or enjoy a game of golf first, and the work waiting in my office can come later. Maximize pleasure, minimize pain. Does anyone else out there have this problem? "Of course not," I say with tongue in cheek.

Seriously, it is altogether too common for us to delay the spiritually important work of maintaining a healthy relationship with God until it suddenly becomes urgent. I wish we would not need a wakeup call such as a serious accident or the onset of cancer to rekindle our flickering flame of faith. But there is true value in those painful experiences which jar our senses, root out our pernicious presumptions, and plant new seeds of seriousness about living the rest of our days in quest of eternal happiness.

"Seventy is the sum of our years, or eighty, if we are strong; most of them are sorrow and toil; they pass quickly, we are all but gone." (Ps 90:10) I have already passed my seventieth birthday, heading toward eighty, at this time of writing. Can I presume on ninety? A hundred?

> Average life expectancy in the United States as of 2023 was 79.74 (77.27 for males and 82.23 for females) In Hong Kong, the longevity leader, it was 85.83, followed by Macao at 85.51 and Japan at 84.95. In Canada it was 83.02, Ireland 82.88, United Kingdom 83.21, and in Mexico 75.04 (ranked 92nd.) The United States was ranked 47th.
>
> While we Americans now lag behind many other countries in life expectancy, we note the general trend of improved longevity in developed nations. India also improved to 72.03 years.[2]

Statistics being what they are, the Psalm quite well expresses the reality of our mortal nature. Hebrews probably did not live that long in the days of King David, author of many of those Psalms. Psalm 90 is attributed to Moses. While we cannot know for sure, it is suspected that many died as children, bringing the average life expectancy down to somewhere between 45 and 50 in biblical times. Those who lived into their thirties, however, could probably be expected to live to 65 or 70.[3]

As to the span of years we may each expect to live, therein lies the great unknown. Just as of the global end times, Jesus says,

> "Heaven and earth will pass away, but my words will not pass away. But of that day and hour no one knows, neither the angels in heaven, nor the Son, but the Father alone. . . Therefore, stay awake! For you do not know on which day your Lord will come.

> Be sure of this: if the master of the house had known the hour of night when the thief was coming, he would have stayed awake and not let his house be broken into. So too, you must also be prepared, for at an hour you do not expect, the Son of Man will come." (Mt 24:36,42-44)

Let not pernicious presumption of another year, another decade, or another quarter century, lull us into complacency about readiness for our personal last days.

---

[1]"Eucharist is 'the source and summit of the Christian Life.'" (*CCC*, 1324, citing Vatican II, *Lumen Gentium*, 11) "The other Sacraments, and indeed all other ecclesiastical ministries and the works of the apostolate, are bound up with the Eucharist and are oriented towards it. For in the Blessed Eucharist is contained the whole spiritual good of the Church, namely Christ himself, our Pasch." (CCC, 1324, citing Vatican II, *Presbyterorum Ordinis*, 5)

[2]https://www.worldometers.info/demographics/life-expectancy:Life Expectancy by Country and in the World (2023)

[3]https://quora.com smartphone search, "What was the average life span of a person in biblical times"

22 Eighth of Nine

We love to attribute nine lives to our furry feline friends who seem to elude so many potentially hazardous encounters, landing upright on their feet after a fall. Humans, on the other hand, are not always so fortunate. In October of 2022, fully a year after my accident, we suffered the tragic loss of one of our young Cooperstown residents. David Lunde, an adventurous 29-year-old, had moved to Colorado a short time before. Early on Saturday morning, the first of October, he had set out on one of the challenging trails to Madden Peak in the San Juan Mountains of the Durango area. The weather deteriorated quickly, as it often can in those mountains. Rain turned to snow, and he never returned from the run. Search parties did their ultimate best but never located David's body.

> "Lunde was an ultra-fit long-distance runner who on the day he disappeared left his apartment on James Ranch where he worked to run a portion of the route known as the La Plata Enchilada. He was training for a six-summit run planned for his 30th birthday on October 23.
>
> Nothing was spared in the effort to locate Lunde. Searchers on foot crisscrossed trails, combed through wooded ravines and valleys, and scoured the summits of multiple peaks. Mounted patrols, dogs, helicopters, drones, and airplanes outfitted with video cameras with software designed to locate people on the ground were all used. Software to locate cellphones and other

> blue-tooth devices was used. And the Air Force Coordination Center provided cellphone location forensics. An estimated 3,462 hours went into the search, according to La Plata County Search and Rescue."[1]

After the second week of unsuccessful rescue efforts, David's sister Kaia Lunde Berggren wrote on her public Facebook group called David Lunde's Prayer Warriors, created a few days after his disappearance:

> "Although our hearts are deeply saddened by this news, we also know our hope isn't in this world. The organizer of the Search and Rescue crew said after the first week, 'We have a boy to bring home.' Although we all prayed fervently for that home to be earth, our family has come to accept that coming home may mean heaven and not on earth."

The article posted in the Dickinson ND Press continues,

> "On October 21, Berggren shared that her brother had planned to run 61 miles to fundraise for Rockside Ranch (a nonprofit residential program for young men) on his 30th birthday, which would have been Sunday, October 23."[2]

A memorial service was held back home in Cooperstown a month following that fateful run, to bring some sense of closure. The family, people of strong faith, handled this tragic and heart-breaking loss with amazing and admirable grace.

Aware of the risks entailed in such endeavors, one of our members texted me on October 17, as we were commiserating over David's situation and I had noted my own proneness to risk-taking adventures: "Yes, Father, you have nine lives and I think you are on 8.5!" Her comment was right on target, insofar as my own gift of more years on earth makes me feel as if I am living on borrowed time.

That comment prompted me to look back on numerous circumstances that could have proven fatal, had their worst-case scenario played out. Unlike the fabled feline, I do not consider nine to be the magic number of death-defying escapes I could be granted. But it intrigued me to review my life and see just how many Houdini-like escapes I could recount. Walking back through the halls of memory, the following escapades came to mind:

When I was very young, my dad would help Grandpa Joe Kapaun with his annual harvest work, and little Dale frequently tagged along. I would ride on daddy's lap on the tractor. I could also watch or get in the way of the rest of the chores. On one occasion when I was only three or four, dad yanked my hand away from the rotating blades of the grain auger. Curious little Dale had extended the fingers of his right hand toward those corkscrew blades carrying newly harvested wheat up into the granary. I could have easily lost a hand, an arm or more, perhaps even a life, that day. I see my dad as the agent of God's grace in that situation. The heavenly Father reached out to save me through earthly father Howard's hands.

Pressing the limits of memory even further back, I recall being in my crib during early childhood, and suffering a bout of whooping cough. Mom had draped the crib with a white sheet, setting up a homemade steam tent to help open my breathing passages. I remember little else but the raspy bark of the croupy cough, the soothing scent of the Vicks VapoRub anointing my chest, and the warm welcome whisper of the steam kettle filling the tent with healing vapors.

> "Whooping cough can cause serious and sometimes life-threatening complications in babies. Many babies with whooping cough don't cough at all. Instead, it causes them to stop breathing and turn blue. About half of babies who get whooping cough

> end up in the hospital. The younger the baby is when (she) gets whooping cough, the more likely it is that doctors will need to treat (her) in the hospital. Of those babies who get treatment in a hospital for whooping cough, about 1 of 4 will get pneumonia and 1 or 2 out of 100 will die. Other complications include violent, uncontrolled shaking, life-threatening pauses in breathing, and brain disease."[3]

I was beyond the baby stage, but just old enough to remember a battle or two with *Bordetella pertussis*, the bacterial invader causing whooping cough. Thanks to expert care from my RN mother Mildred, I escaped without serious harm. I had the other childhood diseases of mumps and measles and chicken pox and tonsilitis all in good time, with no noticeable lasting effects. God has mercifully spared me from any serious adult afflictions of the bacterial or viral kind.

Fast forward now to my adult life. Although relatively healthy and disease-free, I have had my share of risky interactions. Let us first consider my Close Encounters of the Four-legged Kind.

In 1987 I participated in the Headwaters Hundred Mile Bike Ride/Race, held in the beautiful Lake Itasca area of Minnesota. Completing that event successfully, though slower than hoped, I drove homeward in my 1984 Nissan Sentra wagon, relaxed and contented, heading back to the parish I was serving at that time, Saint Alphonsus of Langdon. Twenty-five miles west of Grand Forks on Highway Two, I spied a four-legged hulk emerging from the ditch to my right. Applying the brakes immediately, I barely avoided colliding with a bull moose sauntering nonchalantly across the roadway.

Coming to a complete stop less than twenty feet from the beast, I craned my neck upward, mouth agape, gawking at the ungainly beast with the top of his rack some ten feet above the ground. "Oh my God!" I thought. I was so stunned by the impressive grandeur of the creature, awkward and ugly though he was, it took the better part of a minute to compose myself and resume the journey. Later I realized the possibly fatal consequences of clipping the spindly legs of the moose, causing him to topple onto the windshield or roof of my car. A thousand-to-twelve-hundred-pound animal crashing down on me and my vehicle could have caused serious damage, to say the least.

Then in the year 2000, I was working my way along the Continental Divide Route with my newly acquired mountain bike. I had already done sections farther north, from the Canadian border through central Montana, the previous year. That 1999 episode, by the way, provided my only sighting of a grizzly bear in the wild – a relatively young one bounding downhill into the trees some two hundred yards ahead. Wisely, I resisted the temptation to pursue the creature in quest of a photo worthy of publication in National Geographic.

The mountain biking excursion of 2000 found me trail sampling sections of Wyoming and Colorado, this time using my car as home base. Early one morning I set out on a section of open Colorado rangeland. To my chagrin, a Hereford bull decided to take up residence in the middle of the trail, right where I needed to be. He began pawing the ground with his right hoof, with a low-pitched snort as if to say, "You are not to pass on my turf!" Gingerly dismounting, I backed myself and my metal steed slowly away, still facing the adversary. Cresting the hill behind me, I backed further downhill until I was out of his sight.

Waiting patiently for twenty minutes to a half hour that seemed an eternity, I crept cautiously forward until I could once again see over the crest of that protective hill. Luckily, the bull seemed to have lost interest in me, ambling further down an embankment to my right, apparently intent on drinking from a nearby stream. Seizing the opportunity, I mounted the bike and pedaled quickly yet cautiously forward, heart pounding on overdrive until I was safely past. Pedaling onward without looking back, I prayed I would not hear that ominous snorting sound approaching from behind. All was well. While patiently waiting behind the hill and pondering the possible outcomes, I had envisioned the news headline, "North Dakota Priest Gored by Colorado Bull While Mountain Biking."

As of now, I have never run into a deer while driving. That fact is amazing, given the hundreds of thousands of miles I have logged in prime deer territory. I am careful to slow down during "prime time hours" of evening and night and use my bright headlights wherever possible. Although I have often encountered many potential collisions, I have won the lottery, so to speak, with safe outcomes for each of those encounters.

There was one potentially disastrous occasion involving deer, however. The year was 2018, and I was driving south on Interstate 29, headed for Watertown, South Dakota, where I would meet other priests and couples for a Marriage Encounter enrichment weekend. A highway speed of eighty miles per hour is legal on that stretch in South Dakota, so I took advantage of that fact. I was driving at night in the very same Olds Alero you see on the front cover of this book. While in the act of passing a slower moving truck, my lights showed something ahead in the left lane. I slowed but could not pull over, since the truck was still directly beside me. I certainly could not take the ditch to my left either, since I might roll the vehicle, with serious consequences.

Intuition impelled me to roll directly over the object in question. Split-second decision making is a gift to be treasured in such circumstances.

Not until I was about to hit the object did I realize it was a portion of the hind quarter of a deer that must have already been mangled by a passing truck. In the subzero temperatures of that January night, that hunk of deer must have been frozen solid. Hearing the "Thump!" upon impact, I slowed but kept on driving, to avoid colliding with the truck which was now passing me on the right. Once I had returned to the right lane, caught my breath, and regained my composure, I continued carefully and completed the journey into Watertown. The Alero seemed to be functioning all right, but I resolved to pull in at the first gas station and inspect the potential damage. To my surprise, kneeling down to look under the front bumper, I noticed the chunk of deer was fixed to the radiator, otherwise nothing seemed broken. Attempting unsuccessfully to remove the frozen chunk, I let the car sit at our hotel parking lot all weekend. Then, after driving home all the way to Cooperstown in this condition, I pulled into the warm heated garage to let the Alero and its parasitic attachment reach room temperature overnight.

The next day, I carefully slid the sloppy mess of deer hind quarter from the garage floor into a garbage bag. After consulting with our local sheriff, I drove five miles east to the Sheyenne River Valley bridge and threw the contents of the bag onto the riverbank below, to become coyote food. All the while, I gave thanks to God for guiding me safely through the complex and possibly serious consequences of that car/deer/truck encounter.

So, if you are keeping count, we have two childhood risks and three animal encounters in adulthood. That is five potential losses of life. We might also include, as the sixth, that hiking event in Theodore Roosevelt Park, of which I wrote in the earlier chapter on Fears and Favors, where I carefully worked my way downwind around the buffalo herd resting directly on the trail.

Now, considering the risks of my many athletic endeavors, we can easily count a couple more lives.

Consider, for example, my first attempt at the Ironman Triathlon in 1982. It was a cool Minnesota morning in late August, with an air temperature of 57 degrees at the early morning start. The lake water in which the swimming portion of the event would be held was still warmer, but the cooler air can affect the water surface temperature significantly. I had practiced distance swimming in the YMCA pool in Fargo, but I had not yet mastered the technique of sighting and stroking a straight line in open water. There were no handy lines to follow on the swim course, save for the markers placed every couple hundred yards. They were paired diamond-shaped flags such as you would see on a highway construction project, mounted on buoys. Still naively inexperienced at lake swimming, I would complete twenty-five strokes and then look up to get my bearings. I would readjust my course after each set of twenty-five strokes, finding myself a bit off course each time.

Later, I would learn how to sight every fifth stroke to keep a straight line and swim much more efficiently. But today I was losing time and body warmth in those cooler waters. About half a mile short of the 2.4-mile finish, I heard my lungs begin to rattle. It was the same kind of rattling sound I have heard from the mouths of patients on their death bed. "This can't be good!" I thought to myself. Fortunately, one of the judiciously spaced rescue craft was not far away. I stroked forward to that canoe, hung my right arm over the gunwale, and gasped, "I think you better take me in." They dutifully did so, taking me directly to the medical tent on shore, and wrapped my shivering body in a sleeping bag. The rectal thermometer showed my body temperature had already dropped a couple of degrees. Had I persisted in the swim with dogged determination despite the warning rattle, I certainly would have drowned. Life number six or seven. Or, rearranging our events in chronological order, the buffalo herd was number three, this swimming event number four, followed by the 1987 moose, the 2000 Colorado Bull, and the 2018 South Dakota deer chunk.

Consider another athletic adventure, or two for good measure, and then we can discount the whooping cough. When I moved to Devils Lake in 2007 to assume the pastorate of Saint Joseph Church in that community, I was awestruck by the size of the lake. Several seasons of abundant rainfall had tripled its surface area from its low point in the late 1980's and early 1990's to its high point by the time of my arrival. The Corps of Engineers continued its diking project to save the city and homes in the surrounding area. Maps of the Lake Region reveal some eighty miles of continuous waterway. "This would be a great adventure, to kayak the whole thing from northwest to southeast," I thought.

So, in 2010, I took up this self-assigned challenge. From Cabela's store in East Grand Forks, I purchased a fiberglass kayak, paddles, life vest and accessories. Throughout the course of that summer, I would complete the task, ten miles or so at a time, choosing calm days for each successive leg of the watery journey. Independent as I am, I would drive to the day's finish point, unload my bike, drive to the starting point, unload the kayak, paddle the chosen distance, and bicycle back to the car at the end of the day's outing. All went well until the channel connecting Devils Lake to Stump Lake was all that remained of the eighty miles I was to complete. It was now the Labor Day weekend, and I had decided to launch the kayak on the eastern shore of Stump Lake, work my way westward into the connecting channel, and thus finish traversing the whole waterway with an enjoyably placid ride.

There was just one problem with my plan that day. The morning breeze began to stiffen, but I assumed I could complete the task in time. My trek across the east bay of Stump Lake went fine, since the wind was coming from the south, and I was paddling westward along sheltered shoreline. But upon reaching the main body of the lake, I gasped at the height of the waves the stiffening winds had now stirred up. Before I could decide to abandon, those waves swept me past the loading dock where I could have bailed out. Suddenly I found myself in the middle of the lake, riding the waves like a rodeo cowboy on a bucking bronco. I would slap the water from side to side with my paddle blades to prevent the craft from capsizing.

Legs shaking and knees knocking, I prayed furiously, reciting frantic Our Fathers and Hail Mary's for the better part of ten miles. I could not make my way westward to the calmer waters of the channel, for the south winds and the angry waves would have surely capsized me. All I could do was slap the water with those paddle blades and ride the waves all the way to the north shore. There, thankfully, was a resort, and cabins, and a kind gentleman who met me and offered to drive me back to my car. I would navigate the channel several days later and complete the project. News stories of drowned boaters and kayakers are infrequent, but one is too many, and I could well have been another of those water casualties.

We are now at seven or eight lives, and I could count my accident the 8.5, but I will throw in another for good measure. In 1999 and 2000 I entered in the Pikes Peak Ascent Race, held in Manitou Springs, Colorado. I would drive down early in the week to visit cousins and do some altitude training. On a Wednesday before the Saturday race of 2000, I had trekked all the way up the Barr Trail to the 14,115-foot summit of Pikes Peak. After a bit of rest and refueling with coffee and a donut from the visitor center at the top, I began to work my way down. While still above the tree line, I spied the skies darkening in the west. Suddenly, as often occurs in midafternoon there, the clouds burst open with rain turning to sleet. Lightning scared me into hiding under a large rocky outcropping until the sudden storm had passed. My cousin Deb began to wonder anxiously, what was taking me so long to get back to their house in Colorado Springs. My cell phone did not work up there, so it was not until near the finish of my descent that I could let her know I was okay and would soon be on my way back. So, there is another potential fatality -- being struck by lightning while on that mountain trail.

So, my parishioner friend's text, contending that I am on life number 8.5, seems accurate enough. Come to think of it, if I were to count other near misses and Close Encounters of the Automobile Kind, including the trio of trucks on Interstate 80 I include in the next chapter, I may have already exceeded my theoretical limit of nine. In sum, I must readily admit I have survived more than my share of risky situations. Providentially, thankfully, I have landed cat-like on my feet so far.

But finally, as his sister Kaia said of David Lunde, a safe homecoming will be in heaven and not on earth. Our feet (i.e., our souls) will ultimately come to rest where God intends for them to be, safe in the divine embrace for all eternity. Fully aware of that reality, I most eagerly anticipate a successful landing.

---

[1]Garrett Jaros, Durango Herald, Nov 3, 2022, (https://www.durangoherald.com/articles/celebration-of-life-held-for-missing-durango-runner-david-lunde)

[2]Sav Kelly, "Search Suspended for Missing Colorado Man with North Dakota Ties," The Dickinson Press, Oct 24, 2022, (https://www.thedickinsonpress.com/news/north-dakota/search-suspended-for-missing-colorado-man-with-north-dakota-ties)

[3]https://www.cdc.gov/mom

23 Thumbs Up, Truckers

Yes, there are truck drivers who make errors in judgment, resulting in accidents, often serious or fatal for the driver of a smaller vehicle in the event of collision with one of the big rigs. My accident would be one such example. Fortunately, though my injuries could be considered serious, they were not life-threatening.

Yet the accident responsibility shoe is often on the other foot, where the driver of a smaller vehicle may do something unwise or risky when approaching, meeting, or passing the bigger rig. I had a very fruitful and enlightening conversation with one long-haul truck driver, who in fact happens to be the husband of Sarah, my physical therapist for those many weeks of rehabilitation in Cooperstown. We met during the spring dinner at our St. Lawrence parish hall, and when I learned of his profession, I was eager to hear more from the perspective of the truck driver. He reminded me, and made me more aware, of the many kinds of dangerous stunts we motorists may pull in the presence of semi drivers bringing goods of all kinds to market. We tend to forget the massive weight of those trucks loaded with cargo, and the extra time they need to slow down and come to a stop, as well as the extra room they need in order to negotiate a turn.

I recall encountering one such dangerous situation while driving eastbound on Interstate 80, returning from a visit to friends in the Southwest. It was a wintry day, and there was fresh snow on the highway. Three trucks were entering the roadway from a rest area, one behind the other. Several cars approached this trio from further west and made their bid to pass. I had just taken my turn lining up in queue behind the other passenger vehicles, when another pickup driver decided to try pulling ahead of me, approaching from my right. My latent road rage kicked in, and I held my right hand and outstretched arm toward him to indicate, "Not on my watch, buddy!" Pressing closer to the car ahead of me, I made sure there was no room for that pickup to squeeze me out of my place in line.

All the while, we needed to be aware of the trio of trucks and the potential hazard of passing them in these slushy conditions, let alone on a dry road surface. Any misstep in this situation could have resulted in one of those all-too-frequent multiple vehicle collisions, and one or more fatalities. Fortunately, we all finished the risky negotiation without casualty. Many are not so lucky in similar circumstances.

Reviewing the 2021 statistics, "the National Highway Traffic Safety Administration estimates 42,915 people died in motor vehicle traffic crashes, a 10.5% increase from the 38,824 fatalities in 2020. The deaths include pedestrians, cyclists and others who may have died during a crash."[1]

I know of one bicyclist in particular, whose name is Father Dennis Dempsey, of whose death I wrote in a previous chapter. You may also know one or more of these motorists or cyclists or pedestrians by name. Statistics reveal the problem in general, but individual deaths cause pain in each unique case for family and friends.

Another site gives "Truck accident statistics you should know – important truck accident statistics for all drivers": "Sixty-eight percent of all truck fatalities are passenger vehicle occupants. Furthermore, approximately 130,000 annually suffer from truck accident-related injuries." I know one of those 130,000 by name – Dale Kinzler.

According to NHTSA (National Highway Traffic Safety Administration), fatalities involving large trucks increased by 13% compared to 2020.

> "In 2021, **5,788 people** were killed and nearly 155,000 people were injured in crashes involving large trucks. Since 2009, the number of fatalities in large truck crashes has increased by 71 percent. In the first six months of 2022, traffic fatalities in crashes involving at least one large truck were up 10 percent; 2,811 people were killed. In fatal two-vehicle crashes between a large truck and a passenger motor vehicle, 97 percent of the fatalities were occupants of the passenger vehicle. According to the Insurance Institute for Highway Safety (IIHS), side underride crashes result in hundreds of lives lost and serious injuries each year."

Alex Kopestinsky writes, in "24 Disturbing Truck Accident Statistics" (2022 edition):

> "The trucking industry in the US is consistently on the rise, even though newer and faster means of transport are being invented by the day. Truck transport is considered to be one of the most suitable ways to get goods across the United States, with about 70% of all products reaching their destination via a type of truck. … Regardless, this industry has gained great notoriety over the years, especially in the last couple of decades; with a plethora of careless drivers of such large trucks, accidents are bound to happen. … Truck accident statistics show that among the top reasons for truck accidents are driver's fatigue and inexperience. Because these vehicles are not simple to operate, truck drivers need to be experienced and well-rested before they hit the road to ensure safe vehicle operation and maximum control."[2]

"Commercial truck accident statistics show 97% of all deaths in crashes involving one or more large trucks were from the passenger vehicle – car, van or SUV."[3]

This simply stands to reason, as the little guy is almost always going to come out worst in such encounters.

Truck driver regulations have been enforced to reduce accidents.

> "The truck driver factor in accident statistics has been in the focus of regulations intended to reduce the possibility of crashes. FMCSA restricts the number of hours that truck drivers can spend behind the wheel to 14, and at the same time demand mandatory rests during the drive if there haven't been a minimum of 8 hours since the driver's last haul. Electronic stability control (ESC) has also been enforced to this effect, with initial results from 2011 to 2015 showing that ESC has saved about 7,000 lives."[4]
>
> "Large trucks understandably weigh much more than a regular vehicle, especially when bearing cargo to the maximum. As a result, their total weight oftentimes surpasses 40 tons, as opposed to your regular passenger vehicle that normally weighs about 2.5 tons. Due to such circumstances, these trucks take a lot longer to come to a stop than regular vehicles, and all the more so if their cargo is not loaded evenly and properly in the back trailer." (Source: Isaacs & Isaacs.)
>
> "Tractor-trailer vehicles, due to their massive weight, require a greater stopping distance than a regular passenger one. For example, if the latter would need no more than 300 feet to stop after hitting the brakes, the former would take nearly double the distance – 525 feet more precisely. Speed, mechanical readiness, as well as driver fatigue are also contributing factors to the stopping

> time, which are the common causes of these accidents." (Isaacs & Isaacs)

I share these statistics and statements gathered from smartphone search, simply to remind myself, and you the reader, to respect the truck driver and his or her rig. Drive smart, drive safe, and share the road, giving the truckers the room and the respect they need to conduct their business safely and successfully. Many of the avoidable fatal crashes are not the truck driver's fault. And buckle your seat belt. That discussion comes in the next chapter.

---

[1]https://www.cnbc.com, May 17, 2022

[2]https://policyadvice.net/insurance/insights/truck-accident-statistics

[3]www.legalinfo.com/content/truck-accidents/truck-accident-statistics.html

[4]Source: TruckAccidentAttorneyNetwork.org

24 Blessed Belts and Bags

From my earliest years as a driver, I developed the habit of fastening my seat belt before setting out on the road. Air bags came into being in the 1970s, but my first few cars were not yet equipped with one. So, I wanted to maximize my chances of survival in the event of a crash. I had heard arguments for and against the belt. Some folks told of freakish accidents in which wearing the belt might have resulted in a worse outcome. But in the majority of instances, being thrown from the vehicle or hurled through the windshield is far more likely to result in a fatality.

Fortunately, the driver and passenger airbags were standard equipment in the 2004 Alero I was driving that day, and they were still functional in 2021. I had never actually needed one until that nearly fatal day of September 14. But that airbag, in concert with the fastened seatbelt, was a significant factor in my survival that day. Imagine the consequences, if you will, of the centrifugal force on myself and the car as it was being pushed clockwise into the ditch. My left knee slammed against the door which was also being forced open as the window pillars collapsed along with the collapsing engine compartment. In my mind's eye, I can see myself being hurled outside the car if I were unbelted. I can see my completely broken right leg being further torn apart, the jagged edges of bone rupturing blood vessels and leaving me there to bleed to death.

Now I cannot substantiate whether this would have been the actual outcome were I not belted in, but I can well imagine it happening. The statistics on fatalities where the unbelted driver and/or passengers are thrown from the vehicle are convincing enough for me. The NHTSA report showed 42,915 motor vehicle fatalities in 2021.[1]

> "Seat belt usage was at 89.6%, an 11% increase from 2014 reports. Seat belts saved almost 15,000 lives in the U.S. Seat belts could have saved an additional 2,549 lives. 47% of passengers who died in motor vehicle crashes were not wearing seat belts."[2]

> "The simple act of buckling up can prevent nearly 50% of automobile deaths. More than 75% of people who are ejected during a fatal crash die from their critical injuries. Only 1% of passengers who were wearing a seat belt were ejected from a car during a crash."[3]

Statistics certainly favor buckling up, and that is going to be my practice for the rest of my life. I hope any reader who until now has chosen not to buckle up will reconsider. I don't need a "Click It or Ticket" campaign. I don't need to be pulled over and fined for lack of wearing the belt. My survival that day is incentive enough for me.

---

[1]www.nhtsa.gov/press-releases/early-estimate-2021-traffic-fatalities

[2]nhtsa.gov, December 30, 2021

[3]nhtsa.gov, July 7, 2022

25 Prayer Power

Word of the accident spread fast, through the local grapevine, the Fargo Diocese communication chain, and the local news. WDAY TV aired the story on the 10 pm news that very night, with the picture of the vehicle. So, within eight hours of my injury, hundreds of prayers were lifted heavenward on my behalf. Family, friends, parish members, and Christians of each church in the Cooperstown area all joined in prayerful plea for my healing and recovery. Cards and letters and calls to that effect streamed in over the next three weeks of my PAM Rehab Hospital stay.

"I am lifted up on the wings of your prayers," I would respond to each person who sent notice of their part in the collective effort. My own recitation of the Rosary while in the air on the way to Fargo Sanford Hospital perhaps helped pave the way for the flood of prayers to follow.

Reflecting on the results of my rehabilitation and recovery process, I can attest to the fact that those prayers bore fruit. Determination to do everything I could to play my part in the therapy exercises would be the mental and physical ingredients of the recipe for healing. The power of prayer invoking divine assistance would be the spiritual ingredient, the secret formula as it were. I give full credit to God not only for spilling me from death that day, but for the relatively complete success of the slow and steady healing process I have experienced along the way.

Granted, my recovery was not one of the kind defying the rules of medical science. As I wrote at the beginning of this work, mine was not to be a "pick up your mat and go home" sort of miracle. But it was surely an ongoing work of divine providence and the fruit of prayer.

Recognizing that many more serious injuries, with fatal outcomes, happen daily across our land, I consider myself so fortunate as to have escaped the worst. But what of those who were not so fortunate -- those who, despite the many prayers sent heavenward, died of their injuries?

I can only offer words of consolation, that the prayers of family and friends did not go unheeded. Every prayer we offer bonds us more closely with the One who always hears us. I write these thoughts after having just read the words of the priest Tertullian, as given in our Office of Readings for Thursday of the Third Week of Lent[1]:

> "Since God asks for prayer in spirit and in truth, (cf. Jn 4) how can he deny anything to this kind of prayer? How great is the evidence of its power, as we read and hear and believe. Of old, prayer was able to rescue from fire and beasts and hunger, even before it received its perfection from Christ. How much greater then is the power of Christian prayer. No longer does prayer bring an angel of comfort to the heart of a fiery furnace (Dan 3) or close up the mouths of lions (Dan 6) or transport food from the fields to the hungry. *No longer does it remove all sense of pain by the grace it wins for others. But it gives the armor of patience to those who suffer, who feel pain, who are distressed. It strengthens the power of grace, so that faith may know what it is gaining from the Lord, and understand what it is suffering for the name of God.*"

In prayer we ask whatever God most wills for our well-being in that circumstance, and gratefully accept whatever God gives in response.

"And I tell you, ask and you will receive; seek and you will find; knock and the door will be opened to you. For everyone who asks, receives; and the one who seeks, finds; and to the one who knocks, the door will be opened. What father among you would hand his son a snake when he asks for a fish? Or hand him a scorpion when he asks for an egg? If you, then, who are wicked, know how to give good gifts to your children, how much more will the Father in heaven give the Holy Spirit to those who ask him?" (Lk 11:9-13)

---

[1]*The Liturgy of the Hours*, Vol. II (New York: Catholic Book Publishing Co., 1976), 250

26 Surprised by the Spirit

"Have you noticed any changes in yourself since your accident?" My response to this query is "No, not really." I am essentially the same person as before, with the same personality and behavioral strengths and weaknesses. My unflinching commitment to the prayer of the Liturgy of Hours is the most tangible change I can cite. Along with that comes an increased zeal for prayer, for study and for preaching.

When the Covid-19 pandemic led to church service shutdown in March of 2020, Deacon Wally and I offered Mass at the altar of Saint George Church with absolutely no one in the assembly, save for his wife Colleen. We videotaped the Mass for the rest of our flock and posted it to our newly developed YouTube channel, StGeorge Cooper. Once our people were allowed to return to worship in early May, I experienced "movie-making withdrawal symptoms." So, I went on to develop "Fireside with Father Dale," a weekly video series in which I share fifteen to twenty minutes of reflection from the various commentaries and resource books at my disposal. I pledged to keep up the weekly series, posting it to our YouTube channel, until the day of my retirement.

Over the years, this studiously shy priest gained comfort in public speaking and preaching from the pulpit week after week. Sometimes I script the homily in full detail after reading bible commentaries and other relevant spiritual writings. Other times I will prepare notes with the major points of emphasis. Often, I will preach spontaneously, drawing from current events, personal experience and the storehouse of study already done over the past four dozen years of ministry.

Celebrating daily Mass is the greatest privilege I enjoy as a Catholic priest. Whether the assembly of God's People gathered with me on a particular day is large or small, I will read the Scriptures pre-selected according to the Revised Common Lectionary and provide a homiletic reflection on those Scriptures. We then proceed to share the Liturgy of Eucharist, to be nourished by the Bread of Life in receiving Holy Communion.

Preaching the Word of God is a joyous challenge. Reading the selected Scriptures and reflecting upon them serves as the center of my prayer life. As of September 2021, I had completed almost forty-eight years of ordained ministry. Our Sunday Scriptures follow a three-year cycle, and our daily Scriptures follow a two-year cycle. That means, over the course of four dozen years of preaching, I had reviewed those same Sunday readings sixteen times and weekday readings twenty-four times.

On a given day I can walk into the sacristy, don my vestments in preparation for the Mass, glance at the lectionary to review the readings, and prepare my homiletic thoughts then and there, without having spent time in prayer and study beforehand. I am not advocating that approach, of course. Ideally, I would have arisen much earlier and spent time in prayer over these passages of Scripture. But many days find me engaged in other activities, such that I rush into the sacristy barely in time to begin Mass. In that case I must rely on recall of thoughts I have shared in years past, perhaps two or three years ago, the last time those readings occurred in our lectionary cycle, or even a couple dozen years before that.

On the other hand, I have spent many Saturdays in careful preparation for preaching the Word of God for our people attending Sunday Mass. I will study several commentaries and script the homily to convey the message as precisely, clearly, convincingly, and colorfully as possible. During my years as pastor of Saint Joseph Church of Devils Lake, I would preach from the pulpit while a signer conveyed my message to a hearing-impaired member of our congregation. In case her signer was not there for some reason, I could hand her a copy of my script, so she could also benefit from the message of the day.

My preparation for Sunday preaching in Cooperstown now includes reviewing what I scripted nine or twelve years earlier in Devils Lake. I may use it again as is or modify it to incorporate any new situation arising on the global or local scene, and any new happenings in my own life or that of the community I serve. This, believe, is as it should bc. There are eternal truths to convey, and there are current events to consider, new applications of the Gospel for our daily lives.

I find consolation in Jesus' word following his teaching on the kingdom of heaven in the Gospel of Matthew: He asks, "Do you understand all these things?" They answered, "Yes." And he said to them, 'Then every scribe who has been instructed in the kingdom of heaven is like the head of a household who brings from his storehouse both the new and the old." (Mt 13:51-52)

When I approach the pulpit at daily Mass, I am bringing the new and the old from my mental and spiritual storehouse. What I said years ago may quickly come to mind, so I always have some worthy insight to offer that day. But something interesting happened to me following my experience of being three feet from death on September 14, 2021. Spontaneous thoughts I know I have never shared before will leap to mind, and as I share them, I silently quiz myself, "Now where did that idea come from?"

Let us call it a surprise of the Spirit. Spontaneity is a gift I welcome in those situations. Impromptu speaking is a handy talent, a useful tool for a fellow such as I, who may be called upon to preach or lead a prayer at the drop of a hat. Spontaneous speaking is not new to me. But I have found, in these post-accident days, more previously unthought thoughts and unshared words than ever before. Let me give a couple examples, and then reflect on the source of such surprises.

It was a Saturday morning, and the reading was from Genesis 18, where Abraham and Sarah offer hospitality to three men standing near their tent. One of them says, "I will surely return to you about this time next year, and Sarah will then have a son." Sarah laughs in disbelief, and she lies about her laughter, but the Lord catches her at it. (Cf. Gen 18)

Now, by providential happenstance, this reading was proclaimed by Catherine Larson, one of our faithful lay persons in attendance that morning. She was in her last month of pregnancy, and in fact would give birth only ten days later. As I began my homily, the first words that leapt to mind were, "Bringing a child into the world is no laughing matter for the mother of any age!" At which Catherine and the rest of the small congregation chuckled.

"It's good to be good, and bad to be bad." This laughably trite oversimplification of the Book of Proverbs leapt from my lips one morning while preaching on a passage from that book. In the prescribed selection of readings for our Catholic daily Masses, we read from several chapters in Proverbs during the Twenty-fifth week of Ordinary Time.

I smile at the thought of sharing my simple summary of Proverbs while recalling the prime moral directive from the pen of the great scholastic theologian, Saint Thomas Aquinas: "Love and pursue that which is good; detest and avoid that which is evil."[1]

But the Spirit's surprises are more than catchy words and phrases. I have found the Holy Spirit prompting me to ponder new ways of looking at the "same old" texts I have read sixteen to twenty-four times over. Here is one example:

January 14, 2023, was designated on our liturgical calendar as Saturday of the First Week in Ordinary Time. The Gospel assigned to that day portrayed the call of Matthew, known also as Levi:

> "As he passed by, he saw Levi, the son of Alphaeus, sitting at the customs post. Jesus said to him, 'Follow me.' And he got up and followed Jesus. While he was at table in his house, many tax collectors and sinners sat with Jesus and his disciples, for there were many who followed him. Some scribes who were Pharisees saw that Jesus was eating with sinners and tax collectors and said to his disciples, 'Why does he eat with tax collectors and sinners?' Jesus heard them and said to them, 'Those who are well do not need a physician, but the sick do. I did not come to call the righteous but sinners.'" (Mk 2:13-17)

While proclaiming those verses, a question leapt to mind: "Why did those Pharisees quiz the disciples instead of Jesus himself? Were they too timid or too embarrassed to confront him directly?" We find many direct confrontations later in the Gospels. In this situation, did they want to see whether the disciples had already adopted Jesus' attitude toward those folks perceived to be sinners, whom the Pharisees would strictly shun?

Here we see that Jesus intervenes before the disciples can conjecture a response. Mark tells us Jesus overheard the conversation. Elsewhere we find Jesus knowing their devious thoughts even before they utter a contentious word. He takes this moment as a teaching opportunity, to clarify for the Pharisees, for the disciples, and for us, exactly what the purpose of his mission is. "I did not come to call the righteous, but sinners." So, since we are all sinners, Jesus would choose to sit at table with you and me today as well!

I cannot lay claim to this insight as if it were never shared by any other preacher. It is nothing new in the storehouse of Gospel commentaries. But it was a new thought for Father Dale Kinzler that day. Time and time again, new ideas will pop into my head and new words will find their way to my lips, such that I surprise myself and smile within. I will frequently pause to ponder the Source of that spontaneous thought and give silent credit to its Provider.

A relatively natural explanation complements the credit I give to the Holy Spirit. Ever since my accident, I have spent more time in daily prayer, meditation, and study of the Word. In Sunday homily preparation, I will most often consult respected commentaries such as that authored by William Barclay[2] and the Catholic Commentary on Sacred Scripture.[3]

In the case of these verses from the Gospel of Mark, both sources provide an excellent explanation of the Pharisaic avoidance of those whose livelihood or lifestyle reflects a disregard for either the primary law of God or secondary scribal laws. In Mary Healy's commentary I found:

> "Apparently lacking the courage to confront Jesus directly, they demand an explanation from his disciples. In response, Jesus utters a proverbial saying that gives a crucial insight into his messianic mission: he is a physician and his mission is to heal."[4]

So, the lack of courage on the part of the Pharisees became my focal point for that day's message, even without having consulted her commentary text. While the main point of this passage would be Jesus' choice to associate with those in need of the healing physician of bodies and souls, my focus on the timidity of the scribes led me to reflect on times where my own lack of courage prevented me from confronting a problem situation directly. That was the personal application of the passage I offered my listeners to ponder as well.

Let me share one more example: It was Saturday of the Twenty-first week in Ordinary Time. On that day we finish our sequential reading of the Gospel of Matthew, where we read the Parable of the Talents. (Mt 25:14-30) The Epistle reading was a portion of Paul's First Letter to the Thessalonians:

> "Brothers and sisters, on the subject of fraternal charity you have no need for anyone to write you, for you yourselves have been taught by God to love one another. Indeed, you do this for all the brothers throughout Macedonia. Nevertheless we urge you, brothers and sisters, to progress even more, and to aspire to live a tranquil life, to mind your own affairs, and to work with your own hands, as we instructed you." (I Thess 4:9-11)

I had never made this connection in previous years, but on that day, it occurred to me that the "talents" given to the servants in the Gospel, "to each one according to his ability," could refer not only to our various individual abilities, but also to the life of grace and holiness God entrusts to each one of us, servants of the divine will, to live a virtuous life.

The "first talent," in this mode of thinking, then, would be our knowledge of the natural law, the basis of our Ten Commandments. The awareness of a God to whom we owe our worship and obedience, the realization that we owe honor and respect to our parents and lawful authorities, the respect for the sanctity of life and the property of others, the obligation to tell the truth – all these natural laws are evident to the person of reason guided by faith.

The second talent, in this mode of thinking, could be the life of grace given to us through Baptism, the indwelling of the Holy Spirit and our discipleship in the way of Jesus Christ. By faithfully investing these gifts of grace, we are rewarded when the master settles accounts with us: "Come, share your master's joy."

The ones with five talents, then, would be those living in extraordinary holiness such as we see in the example of the saints. By living their gifts to the fullest, they receive the highest honor for having doubled the master's investment, yet their final reward is the same: "Come, share your master's joy."

In the parable the person given one talent, however, buries it in fear of its loss. In the mode of thought I was pursuing in this reflection, that would be the person who refuses even to follow the most basic prompting of conscience, rejecting and violating the dictates of the natural law. Sadly, all too many who subscribe to purely secular and godless ways of thinking, subject to anti-Christian worldviews, will fall into this category. They are the ones most likely to hear the master's rebuke, "Throw this useless servant into the darkness outside, where there will be wailing and grinding of teeth."

Now my reflection on Matthew 25:14-30 in connection with I Thessalonians 4:9-11 is not necessarily found in scholarly commentaries on those passages. But I share this personal reflection as an example to encourage our readers to spend time "bathing in the word," to spiritually soak in the warmly refreshing waters of meditation on Bible passages of your choosing, or the designated readings of the day. Commentaries can help to keep you on the right track, but you can rely on God's Holy Spirit to direct you toward surprisingly delightful discoveries.

In the case of this example, I later consulted the Catholic Commentary on Sacred Scripture and found a similar thread of thought:

> "Being entrusted with the message of salvation entails great responsibility. To sit on the message or bury it for ourselves is a serious breach of responsibility to the Lord, who calls us to share his good news with the world. … Only by investing our gifts and turning a profit for the Lord will we enter into the joy of his kingdom."[5]

As part of my renewed zest for study and prayer on the Scriptures, I became an enthusiastic follower of the highly popular series titled "The Chosen." Millions have tuned in to view this series on the life of Jesus and his call of the apostles.[6]

I delight in the insight and creativity the series provides. The producers have obviously done extensive research and careful preparation of the script to help stimulate our imaginations as to how life for these disciples, and for Christ himself, might have gone, to help us "read between the lines" of the Gospel. I began viewing the series in the summer of 2022, during some of my extra reflection times. Those episodes have fueled my own imagination and appreciation of the life of the chosen twelve and the other significant figures we find in the Gospel accounts. New treasure to add to the storehouse of heart and mind from which some of those seemingly spontaneous thoughts may spring to the lips of this homilist.

The portrayal of the character of Matthew in The Chosen I have found delightful. He comes across to the viewer as a young, timid, obsessive-compulsive fellow who needs a Roman official to stand guard at the customs post while he collects the taxes from behind the safety of a sturdy wooden grill. In the made-for-screen first episode of Season 3, the tension between Matthew (Levi) and his father Alphaeus is very evident. They have an opportunity for reconciliation later in the film. Scenes from the film flashed before me as I read from the Gospel on the call of Matthew Levi at our morning Mass, and visions of the quizzical Pharisees danced in my head.

Practice Makes Perfect

We whose vocation entails preaching are continually enriched by the research, reflection, and prayer we do. By way of analogy, professional golfers devote countless hours of disciplined practice so they can face a challenging shot with confidence based on previous experience in similar circumstances. Similarly, the better I stock my storeroom with treasures of spiritual insight, the better prepared I will be to deliver a fruitful message each day.

I will add one more example, a Spirit-surprise I had while celebrating the Mass of Monday, May 1, 2023. The first of May is dedicated to Saint Joseph the Worker. But his memorial is now optional, so the readings of Monday of the Fourth Week of Easter were given priority. The day before, the Fourth Sunday of Easter, is known as "Good Shepherd Sunday" because we always read verses from the tenth chapter of the Gospel of John, in which Jesus identifies himself as the Good Shepherd. That day we had read verses 1 through 10. Then on Monday we read the next verses:

> "I am the Good Shepherd. A good shepherd lays down his life for the sheep. A hired man, who is not a shepherd and whose sheep are not his own, sees a wolf coming and leaves the sheep and runs away, and the wolf catches and scatters them. This is because he works for pay and has no concern for the sheep." (Jn 10:11-13)

By coincidence this reading fell on the day of Saint Joseph the Worker, always observed on May 1. While Deacon Wally was proclaiming the

Gospel, a new connection leapt to mind. In the homily, I referred to Saint Joseph as an example of one whose work in carpentry put food on the table, while his primary vocation was that of shepherd of the Holy Family. He was no hireling. He laid down his life, not exactly in the kind of sacrificial death Jesus suffered for us, but in the daily sacrifice of his labors, his care, and his purity of love for the Blessed Mother and her Son.

Amazing and amusing, the only persons attending our 5:30 pm Mass at St. George Church that day were Deacon Wally and his wife Colleen, a retired teacher who was still substituting on many days. There was one other person in the assembly that day, Pauline Kenninger, a retired lady who is very active in the parish Altar Society. So, there we were, one priest nearly ready to retire, a deacon who performs his ministry on a volunteer basis, a working retiree and one who volunteers many hours of work within the parish community. I could see in each of us a care for the flock of God's People, who do what we do, laying down our lives in unique ways for the good of others, without regard for the wage. The work we do flows from our primary vocation as members of the household of believers, as labors of love.

Beyond the surprise of new preaching insights, an even more delightful surprise is the initiative of parish members seeking growth in their relationship with Christ. Without my prompting or pleading, two groups of women's bible study formed over the past two years. In November of 2022 they organized, on their own initiative, a wonderful evening of reflection called "Reigniting Our Faith," for ladies of the community, with dinner and two guest speakers, in preparation for the Advent Season. Over seventy-five area ladies filled the Hannaford Mercantile event center for the occasion. That is a remarkable turnout for a small community such as ours.

Then another man of the parish, an active member of our Knights of Columbus Council, came forward at one of the meetings and asked, "Why can't we start a men's group?" My answer, as best I can recall, was "There's no reason we can't, if you are willing to get it going." That he did, and we have been meeting every other Wednesday for the past several months. We have a study topic, discussion, and intercessory prayer time. I had been hoping and praying for something like this but never quite knew how to start one myself, since I had run out of steam after experiencing limited attendance for any of the Lenten programs I had put together on my own initiative.

Although the accident and the effects of aging have necessitated a re-evaluation of my physical capabilities, I continue to enjoy the musings of a relatively agile mind. Retiring from active ministry does not mean the end of priestly service for me. Simultaneously trembling and tickled at the thought of moving on into retirement, I am delighted to live one more day and one more year, eager to see what surprises the Holy Spirit holds in store.

Similarly, anyone who retires after many years of employment, whether continuing to perform work of any kind or not, is still engaged in living the primary vocation of discipleship. Following the call of Christ, listening to the voice of the Good Shepherd, is a lifetime occupation. And our retired seniors, individually and collectively, have so much wisdom to offer our next generation in faith-filled response to the challenges our world presents.

> "If you love me, you will keep my commandments. And I will ask the Father, and he will give you another Advocate to be with you always, the Spirit of truth, which the world cannot accept, because it neither sees it nor knows it. But you know it, because it remains

with you, and will be in you. I will not leave you orphans; I will come to you." (Jn 14:15-18)

As members of the Church founded by Jesus Christ, we can rely on the help of the Holy Spirit, trusting the Lord will walk with us through our darkest valleys, leading us to green pastures, beside restful waters, and a final dwelling place in his house for years to come. (Cf. Ps 23, Jn 14:1-6) You can expect to be delightfully surprised along the way.

---

[1]I-II, 94,2 as cited in Kreeft, *Summa of the Summa* (Ignatius Press, 1990), 515: "The first principle in the practical reason is one founded on the notion of good, viz., *that good is that which all things seek after.* Hence, this is the first precept of the law, that *good is to be done and pursued, and evil is to be avoided.*

[2]Daily Study Bible Series (Westminster Press, Philadelphia, PA, 1975)

[3]Peter Williamson and Mary Healy, eds., *Catholic Commentary on Sacred Scripture* (Grand Rapids, MI: Baker Academic)

[4]Healy, The Gospel of Mark (Grand Rapids, MI: Baker Academic, 2008), 59-60

[5]Curtis Mitch and Edward Sri, *The Gospel of Matthew* (Grand Rapids, MI: Baker Academic, 2010), 324

[6]Cf. https://www.angel.com/watch/the-chosen

27 Sacred Scars, Wondrous Wounds

Viewers of the 2004 Mel Gibson film, "The Passion of the Christ," will vividly recall the most gruesome scenes, among which are the portrayal of Jesus' scourging and crucifixion. A later scene shows the soldier piercing Christ's side, and the gush of blood and water showering the soldier's face. The final scene shows Jesus emerging from the tomb on Sunday morning, leaving the wrappings behind, the nail hole in his right hand clearly visible.

Go back in time with me now, if you will, to the land of Israel and the day of Jesus' resurrection from the dead. That very evening he would appear to the disciples huddled together in their locked upper room, where just three days before he had shared his Last Supper with them. As recorded in John, the risen Jesus stood in their midst, said "Peace be with you," and showed them his hands and his side. Thomas, who was not among them on this occasion, said "Unless I see the mark of the nails in his hands and put my finger into the nail marks and put my hand into his side, I will not believe." (Jn 20:25)

A week later Jesus reappeared, and this time Thomas was there. Jesus, who knew what Thomas had demanded, invited him to do exactly that, and "be not unbelieving, but believe." Whereupon Thomas touched the wounds and exclaimed, "My Lord and my God." For Thomas, the ability to touch the very marks of the wounds Jesus suffered on Calvary resolved his doubts about the Savior's resurrection. Jesus reminds us, and all who were not there that day,

"Blessed are those who have not seen and have believed." (Cf. Jn 20:19-29)

Human beings, composed of body and soul, are "sacramental" by nature. We benefit greatly from visible signs confirming the invisible realities we experience. Like Thomas, we tend to be skeptical. These days especially, we want to avoid the multitude of scams afoot in our world. The streetwise individual may do well to say, "I'll believe it when I see it."

But the soul open to love and grace, realities invisible to the naked eye, readily perceives these realities and recognizes their effects. We see their fruits in the acts of loving kindness, patience, and gentleness we share with one another. Seeing human beings, God's own handiwork, behaving in a godly manner makes the existence of the Supreme Being more credible. The wounds Christ suffered on our account manifest most wonderfully the Perfect Love at work in our world. We can believe in God's love because we have seen it, up close and personal, through the eyewitnesses who record the events of Jesus' life in the four Gospels.

Humans, bodily beings as we are, understandably spend a good deal of time and energy on physical maintenance. Proper nutrition, rest, exercise, and health care are good and worthy means of personal stewardship.

Beyond the essentials of personal care, there are luxuries we may or may not enjoy. Vanity leads many on a quest for the fountain of youth. The cosmetics industry can thank us for acting on such natural inclinations. While some may spend very little, others may dedicate excessive amounts of time and money to appearance, spending a veritable fortune to forestall the visible effects of the aging process. Cosmetic surgeries can often help reverse some of that inevitable sagging and wrinkling we so dread, but ultimately it matters not how good we look when lying in our coffin.

While I spend far less than the national average on cosmetic products, I share in that concern for external appearance. Over the course of the several months following the accident, I monitored the slow and steady healing of the surgical scars on my right leg and left knee. Natural healing processes are amazing. After removal of the stitches, my wounds continued to close, and the skin's appearance improved dramatically. By the fourth month following surgery, my left leg showed only slight scars on the kneecap and the site of insertion of the plate securing bone fragments beside the knee. My right leg, meanwhile, retained a darker scar extending across the fracture site on the shin at midcalf and a lighter scar at the point of insertion of the hardware serving as an internal walking cast.

In mid-April I decided to try one of the scar gels available at our local pharmacy. I added Vitamin E oil to the daily applications, in hopes of further reducing those scars. Spring and summer found me sitting in the sunlight for extended periods of time, thinking the scars might be less noticeable on darker, tanned skin.

While expending time and energy on appearance, I began to reflect on the value of those lingering scars. I realized the worth of these reminders of the whole experience of suffering and recovery. Why should I want to eliminate them for the rest of my remaining years on earth? On the contrary, I could use them for "show and tell" with anyone who might inquire into any lasting effects of my injuries. Consideration of the wounds and their scars might well lead to discussion of my gratefulness to God for sparing me from death that day, and for the relatively complete recovery I enjoy.

I had already accepted lasting scars from previous surgeries. At age fifteen I suffered a fractured right radius and ulna, the bones of the forearm, while engaged in a high school wrestling match. I wrote of that accident in the earlier chapter. My forearm bears a lengthy scar from the surgical incision to set the bones in place, and my right elbow is scarred at the point of insertion of a temporary rod. Those forearm and elbow scars remind me of the whole event.

Speaking of pain, that momentary intense pain upon removal of the rod from my arm sharpens my awareness of the intense pain Jesus must have felt when the soldiers drove spikes through his hands and feet to fix him to the Cross on Calvary, followed by the extended hours of suffering to his moment of death. Thankfully, I was anesthetized during the whole process of surgical repair and insertion of the rod on the day of the fracture. No anesthesia for Jesus, only a wine-soaked sponge. (Cf. Mt 27:48; Mk 15:36; Jn 19:29-30)

After the car accident of September 14, 2021, I could begin to identify with Jesus' suffering as I lay in my hospital bed for the first forty-eight hours following my accident on the Feast of the Holy Cross. Pain attacked multiple areas of my body, from throbbing headache to distended abdomen to fractured leg, torn knee and cracked pelvis and sprained wrists. In this condition I could more closely identify with the Savior's scourging and crowning with thorns and crucifixion. Thankfully, my suffering was not to end in death, but rather was the beginning of my recovery.

The persistent question, "Can you rate your pain on a scale of 1 to 10?" both amused and frustrated me. I must have started at 9.8 on September 14, and improved to a 3 or 4 by the time I was released from PAM Rehab Hospital three weeks later. Can you imagine the Roman executioners asking Jesus to rate his pain? Their whole purpose was to maximize pain, not to relieve it as was the goal of the hospital staff.

In 2007 I yielded to surgical repair of severely deformed toes. Dr. Arness drilled into each toe and inserted pins to fix them straight. Six weeks later he removed the pins, but light scars on each toe remind me of that repair. If I have learned to live with these, I can certainly learn to live with a few more new scars, considering them "notches on my pistol" recalling life's risky adventures. They also remind me of my vulnerable mortal condition.

The wounds still visible on the hands and side of the crucified and risen Christ, witnessed by the Apostles, remind us of the great love with which he suffered and died. The wounds our military service personnel bring home from their engagement in overseas conflicts tell the story of similarly selfless acts of love for others. These, too, are sacred scars reminding us of the Christlike love enabling their sacrifice.

The movie and television stars of decades ago, beautiful, and handsome as they appeared on screen, give witness to the truth of our physical mortality. Without exception, the ravages of age leave their marks on face and skin. But is there truth in the adage, "Beauty is only skin deep?" I contend that depends on which kind of beauty we are talking about. Beneath our skin there lies a deeper beauty within the human spirit.

The human soul whose well-being is preserved by the gift of divine grace enjoys matchless beauty. Each one still bears the scars of the original sin of our first human parents. We suffer the consequences of a "darkened intellect and weakened will" lessening our power to resist temptation, leaving us prone to personal sin. Our sinful choices deprive us of the beautiful glory God intends for us. If our spiritual scars were more visible, we might be collectively more serious about healing the wounds of sin. But by divine grace, the gift of baptism and the reconciliation of our sins, that beauty of soul is regained and preserved. The deepest beauty of the human person will outlast our bodily corruption in the grave.

In the Apostles' and Nicene Creeds, we profess our belief in the resurrection of the body to life everlasting. Our immortal souls will once again be joined with a bodily dwelling the likes of which we have not yet seen. Others may still recognize our facial appearance and the features they came to know during this lifetime. But just imagine being even healthier than we were in the prime of life. That is essentially what we may experience in our glorified bodies. It is a reality affirmed by those who have experienced near-death glimpses of the Eternal.

Take, for example, the experience of little Colton Burpo, as related in the book by his father, Heaven Is for Real, and as seen in the movie based on the book.[1] Colton describes his meeting with Jesus, and further on, his meeting with "Pop," his maternal grandfather who had passed away in 1975 before Colton was born. In the chapter, "No One Is Old in Heaven," Todd Burpo writes:

"Dad, nobody's old in heaven," Colton said. "And nobody wears glasses."

That was Colton's reaction upon seeing a picture of Pop at age sixty-one. And then, seeing a photo snapped much earlier in 1943, showing mom as a baby girl, and "Pop, a handsome fellow, twenty-nine years young":

> He took the picture from my hand, looked down, and then looked at me, eyes full of surprise. "Hey!" he said happily. "How did you

get a picture of Pop?"

The fact that the Pop Colton said he spent time with was no longer sixty-one but somewhere in his prime, seemed to us a good news/bad news scenario: The bad news is that in heaven, we'll still look like ourselves. The good news is, it'll be the younger version.

Based upon the premise that we will be given that younger version of ourselves, free of physical defects, I hope to meet the twenty-eight-year-old Howard Kinzler in heaven, looking as he did in the December 1943 photo of that handsome serviceman dressed in his Army uniform, arm in arm beside twenty-six-year-old Mildred in her bridal dress. And should there be a mirror, I would expect to see the reflection of a handsome young twenty-five-year-old newly ordained priest as he appeared in 1974, needing no glasses or contact lenses or hearing aids.

The wrinkles and defects we accumulate with age, rather than being feared, may be embraced as the sacred scars of senior citizens, well-earned signs of wisdom and experience.

"He who knew no sin became sin for us, so that we might become the righteousness of God." (2 Cor 5:21) Taking upon himself our human condition, Christ remained sinless, yet bore the consequence of sin on our behalf. He who is both divine and human is the only One capable of offering the ultimate sacrifice that redeems all humanity, thereby healing the wounds of our sin. The divine and sinless Son of God accepted the lot of a common criminal, sentenced to death by crucifixion under Roman rule.

"He himself bore our sins in his body upon the cross, so that, free from sin, we might live for righteousness. By his wounds you have been healed." (I Pt 2:24) This is another way of saying Jesus "became sin for us." His were the physical wounds and the scars, but ours were the sins that wounded him. He is the Lamb of sacrifice, offered to the Father in expiation for our sins. He accepted the penalty deserved by all of us who committed these offenses.

We remain a spiritually wounded and scarred humanity. But the Sacred Scars, the Wondrous Wounds of Christ, reveal the great potential of healing for all who suffer spiritual injury. Nature's way of healing broken skin gives a glimpse of the far greater capacity of the grace of God to heal the wounds of the broken soul.

Beneath the surface of our skin there often lie less visible but even more significant scars of the emotional kind. Many are the victims of physical and verbal abuse in the home or workplace. Many, too, are the victims of sexual abuse by extended family or those in leadership roles. These painful experiences leave lasting scars, and their victims need ongoing therapy, counseling, prayer, and loving support. Time and money spent toward healing these inner wounds is well worth the effort.

In the very last verses of the Book of Proverbs we read, "Charm is deceptive and beauty fleeting; the woman who fears the Lord is to be praised. Give her a reward for her labors, and let her works praise her at the city gates." (Prov 31:30-31)

Men and women alike do well to heed this scripture. Fear of the Lord, and all the spiritual gifts preserving our holiness, take primacy over preservation of physical beauty and handsomeness. Working faithfully at the city gates of our own calling, we may be assured of the just reward of our labors.

In the section of Isaiah referred to as the Suffering Servant songs, we read:

> "There was in him no stately bearing to make us look at him, nor appearance that would attract us to him. . . Yet it was our infirmities that he bore, our sufferings that he endured, while we thought of him as stricken, as one smitten by God and afflicted. But he was pierced for our offenses, crushed for our sins, upon him was the chastisement that makes us whole, by his stripes we were healed." (Is 53:2-5)

These verses clearly apply to Jesus of Nazareth, disfigured as he was by the scourging, the crowning with thorns, and the falls he endured upon bearing the cross to his place of execution.

If I let my own scarred legs remind me of my pains of injury and the process of recovery, then I will not forget the merciful act of divine intervention sparing me from death on the day of my accident. I may continue to apply scar gels and Vitamin E oil and sit in the healing rays of sunshine. But more importantly, I want to yield my scarred soul to the healing oil of the Holy Spirit in repentance for any lingering habits of sin and bask in the Divine Presence of the Son of God. This "Son bathing" takes the form of daily prayer, reflection on the Word of Sacred Scripture, and celebration of the Holy Sacrifice of the Mass. In godly use of my time and energies, my scars may become sacred too.

We must not fear to present ourselves to God with our wounds of body, mind, and soul. Practice the boldness of faith that prompted the woman afflicted with a twelve-year hemorrhage to approach Jesus and touch the tassel of his cloak. Sensing her courageous trust, he turned to her and said, "Daughter, your faith has saved you, go in peace." (Cf. Lk 8:43-48)

If we show our wounds to Christ and allow the grace of his healing presence to penetrate the depths of our soul, we may recover wholeness and the beauty deep within our being, the fullness of the divine image in which we were fashioned. (Cf. Gen 1:27) For this spiritual healing, for the preservation of the eternal youth of every soul, Christ bore the wondrous wounds of the Cross.

Consider Sts. Francis of Assisi and Padre Pio of Pietrelcina, two examples among many who experienced the stigmata, the marks of the wounds of Christ, on their own bodies. These wondrous wounds were a gift bringing them into deeper union with Christ, serving as a reminder of Christ's own suffering for us all. Such occurrences of stigmata are rare, while most of us bear scars from wounds of many sorts. And all, as senior citizens, will bear inevitable changes in appearance and progressive limitations of physical mobility, as our share of the collective wounds of sinful humanity. If we accept them in union with the Suffering Servant, ours too may become wondrous wounds and sacred scars of heavenly healing.

---

[1]Todd Burpo, Heaven Is for Real (Nashville: Thomas Nelson, 2010)

28 Healing Humor

I swear God has a sense of humor. Unlike my dry witticisms of the tongue-in-cheek sort, the divine humor, I believe, is purposeful and not whimsical. Let me clarify with a couple examples in the case of my accident and recovery process.

First, consider my plans to hike the entire Appalachian Trail immediately upon retirement at the end of June in 2024, with the lofty goal of completing a southbound hike of 2200 miles from Maine to Georgia within the five-month period from July through November. I could just imagine God saying with a smile, "I am going to take that unrealistic plan off the table for you. This accident will serve as a perfect opportunity for you to reconsider, to shorten up your hike and still enjoy the experience."

With that purposeful sense of humor, God must have also let me experience what it is like to be the cause of another person's injury. It would put the shoe on the other foot, allowing me to feel something of the emotional agony the driver of the truck causing my injuries must have felt. It would give me solidarity in suffering of another sort, the mental suffering born by much of humankind.

It was August of 2022, nearly a full year following my accident. I had driven to central Oregon to visit former Fargo parish friends who currently lived on a golf resort on the eastern edge of the Cascades. That morning, I was part of a foursome engaged in a round of golf. We had finished the first hole without incident. Hole number two was a scenic par five featuring a right-angle dog leg to the right. From the tee box we looked down some three hundred yards to the bend. Steep pine-and-aspen-covered hills stood guard on either side of the fairway. We were paired as riders on two electric golf carts. Each of us launched our drives into the valley between those hills. All four of us, as senior citizens, would need our second shot to reach the dog leg. My partner, the driver of our cart, had hit safely, landing his ball in perfect position in the middle of the dog leg.

Here, for the sake of privacy, I will use assumed names. Let my cart partner be Curt, and his two friends in the other cart be Frank and Ernest.

Frank and I had mishit our second shot to the right, leaving our balls on the slope of the hill. I thought I may as well take our cart over hillside to begin the search for my ball. While engaged in that process, I heard Ernest, still behind me, shout "Father!" to catch my attention, needing me to move the cart so he could take his second shot. Looking over my left shoulder to watch him, I turned the cart to my right to get out of his line. I had forgotten Frank was standing nearby on the hill. Curt and Ernest began shouting at me to warn me of that situation. In horror, I watched myself and my cart roll downhill right over Frank. I was braking desperately but unable to prevent rolling completely over him, pinning him underneath.

Operating under a huge rush of adrenaline, I put my hands under the right rear quarter of the cart and lifted it a few inches off the ground and yelled to Curt and Ernest to pull him out from underneath. As they did, I was blurting out, "I am so sorry! I am so sorry! I am so sorry!" They stood Frank up and supported him on their shoulders, like team members walking an injured football player off the field. Ernest drove him to the emergency room of the local hospital. Curt and I returned our cart and came just a bit later to the hospital waiting room to check on the status of our injured friend.

Frank had sustained five broken ribs, a fractured sternum, and a broken right ankle. Ernest apprised us of the situation, and assured me, "He doesn't blame you. These things happen, he says, and he knows you did not do it intentionally."

Nonetheless, I was a basket case of emotional self-punishment for the next several days. I did act quickly to call our diocese officials and sought help in reaching our insurer, Catholic Mutual, to initiate a claim for the injury. Their representative was most helpful that day, and throughout the entire process of following up with the injured player. He offered a very pastoral approach in working with Frank and with myself. Surprisingly, I learned the injury victim seemed more worried about how I was doing emotionally than he was about himself physically.

Our Catholic Mutual Insurance representative continued his pastoral approach, keeping in frequent contact with Frank, taking care of expenses as appropriate, and suggesting I keep in contact as well. I did so through periodic calls to Curt who had arranged the outing, as well as a call or two to the recovering man. Ironically, Frank still conveyed his concern for how I was doing, though his injuries were physically troublesome enough. His attitude was so positive throughout the process, it reminded me of my own attitude of gratefulness for being alive to golf another day.

I would never blame God for setting up this situation, but I sense he allowed it to happen, as the occasion for me to learn another lesson in compassion. Having initially punished myself emotionally for days on end, I now knew the grief and remorse felt by those who unintentionally cause suffering in others.

Fortunately, by providential happenstance, I had ready access to counseling for my own post-traumatic stress in this case. One of the staff of Redeeming Grace Counseling in Fargo contacted me shortly after this incident. She informed me they had a new intern and were looking for clients. Might I wish to refer anyone from any of my parishes who could benefit from sessions with the intern? I pondered the offer, then thought I should refer myself for starters, while thinking of other possible referrals.

That proved to be a very wise choice. As God's healing humor would have it, the intern was someone whom I already knew from interaction in previous ministry work. I found the sessions, both in person and online, to be very helpful in working through my feelings regarding this situation as well as a few other concerns I was dealing with at the time.

In fact, I urge any of our readers suffering symptoms of PTSD, or other mental and emotional stresses, to seek counseling help. We may attach more stigma to injuries of the mind than those of the body, but I believe care of our mental health is equally important as care of our physical well-being. I saw the healing humor of the divine at work in my life during the whole process I have just described.

Then, adding to the healing humor of that situation, I had my first face-to-face encounter with the September 14 truck driver about two months after my golf cart incident. One of my elderly parish members had passed away, and guess who was named as one of the six pall bearers! I asked our funeral director to help me identify which of the six he was. Walking up to him before the funeral Mass, I introduced myself and extended my hand in greeting. It was an awkward moment, to say the least, but I felt an opening of the door of reconciliation.

Purposeful divine humor allowed me this moment of positive interaction, I wager. Knowing I could stand upright and walk quite decently then and there, rather than having been laid in a coffin the year before, had to be a relief for him, just as it was for me to know the fellow golfer was improving as we spoke. I had told those aware of the golf cart accident that I would rather suffer another physical injury than be the cause of another person's pain. The sharp pains of the emotional kind were harder for me to bear than those I suffered during my time in Sanford Hospital and the PAM Rehabilitation Hospital.

Attending basketball games of our local high school boys and girls is an important public relations activity for our small-town clergy. In early January of 2023 I was attending one of those games in the Griggs County High School gym. There on the sidelines, enthusiastically shouting words of support to the players, was the farmer-owner of the semi rig, the man who had leaned into my crushed Alero and exclaimed, "I've called 911. They are on the way. Hold on!"

By providential happenstance, the attorney representing WSI, Workforce Safety Insurance, had just finished working with me to reach final terms of my claim settlement. So, I took the initiative to introduce myself to the farmer at halftime of the ballgame. He expressed his relief at seeing how well I was doing, and I updated him with the simple declaration, "I think we are all square."

On March 1, not two months later, I received another call from our Catholic Mutual claims representative. He informed me that he had finished reaching a mutually agreeable settlement with the injured golfer. As he suggested, I called Frank myself that evening and offered my thanks for his positive attitude throughout this process. We exchanged some golfing banter, compared our lingering injury limitations, and even quipped an agreement that, should we meet again, I will not be driving the cart! I learned he was back to golfing but still struggling with limited ankle flexibility. So, I described to him one of the exercises my therapist had suggested for my ankles, in which you scribe the twenty-six letters of the alphabet with your toes. He appreciated the suggestion, and closed with the comment that he couldn't think of anyone better to work with on this injury than our claims representative and myself. I thanked him in turn for being so understanding.

Sadly, "Curt," my cart partner, passed away a year later from a heart attack suffered while walking his dog. God rest his soul and grant him eternal happiness.

There are plenty of situations where, in case of catastrophic injury, courts may be justifiably involved in reaching financial settlements. Neither I nor our fellow golfer saw a need to do this in our cases. We both perceived the most Christian thing to do was to refrain from seeking larger settlements.

> "Settle with your opponent quickly while on the way to court with him. Otherwise your opponent will hand you over to the judge, and the judge will hand you over to the guard, and you will be thrown into prison. Amen I say to you, you will not be released until you have paid the last penny." (Mt 5:25-26)

> "Do to others whatever you would have them do to you." (Mt 7:12)

Healing of wounded relationships is generally more complicated than healing the wounds sustained in vehicle injuries. It may take longer and require much greater effort. But I am betting God smiles upon every effort we make to use the opportunities he sets before us with healing in mind.

29 Go for the Gold: The Marathon That Matters

On November 16 of 2022 I made one of my regular visits to Gretchen Baird Kottke, a member terminally ill with cancer that had invaded her hip region, causing serious pain and difficulty in walking. She was already enrolled in hospice care and was now contemplating a move from her own household to our local Griggs County Care Center.

I listened attentively as she shared her anxiety over this decision, then affirmed the wisdom of this choice for her sake. The dying process is never easy, nor are the steps of regression we experience along the way. She had been initially diagnosed with lung cancer shortly after Easter of the previous year, and gone to Olympia, Washington, for treatment. There she could stay with family and friends and rely on them for transportation to and from appointments.

Her brother Dale Baird had called me from Olympia that mid-November day, having just returned home from an extended visit here in Cooperstown. She was already limited in mobility, rarely leaving her house save for brief trips to the store and medical appointments. Now, laying on her couch in pain, she shared her dilemma, wondering whether to accept this further step in the dying process. She referred to this journey of suffering as a marathon.

That statement opened the door for me, an experienced marathon runner, to carry that analogy a bit further. Nodding in agreement with her comment, I likened her present situation to that point in the race where the runner "hits the wall," a reality I experienced in many of my marathon races. Somewhere between the eighteenth and twentieth mile my stores of glycogen (carbohydrate fuel) would be depleted, causing a distressing slowdown in pace and a serious mood change from euphoric to discouraged. It took sheer determination, my slower-burning fat reserves, and whatever liquid fuel I could still ingest, to push forward to the 26.2-mile finish line from that point onward.

I likened her anxiety over this nursing home decision to hitting her marathon wall physically and emotionally. Already exhausted from the rigors of battling the invading cancer, she would need this specialized help to push forward to her inevitable finish line. She had received wonderful help from volunteer friends and home health care nurses, and the assistance of Red River Valley Hospice. I reinforced the idea that having the personnel right at hand in the care center to offer the needed nutrition, personal care and pain management would be even better than trying to make a go of it in her own home at this point.

I assured her, "Tough as the next few miles of the journey will be, you will win your medal at the finish line." She knew exactly what I meant, and I could see she was translating the analogy, applying its physical and spiritual implications to her own situation.

It is often hard to admit we are dying, but I knew she was aware of her terminal condition, having already declined further treatment alternatives. Barring any truly miraculous recovery, she was bound to reach her bodily finish line soon and very soon. But she was also a woman of strong faith, enabling her to continue her personal marathon with resolve, with the blessed assurance of eternal happiness at the end of her life journey.

As a prelude to offering her the Real Presence of Christ in Holy Communion that day, I offered these words from the Sunday Gospel we had read at Mass the very day before:

> "When some people were speaking about how the temple was adorned with costly stones and votive offerings, Jesus said, 'All that you see here – the days will come when there will be not left a stone upon another stone that will not be thrown down . . . but not a hair on your head will be destroyed. By your perseverance you will secure your lives.'" (Cf. Lk 21:5-19)

I suggested the bodily temple we enjoy for this brief lifetime comes toppling down relatively soon, but we, a "temple of living stones," (cf. I Pt 2:5) are blessed with the indwelling of the Holy Spirit in an immortal soul. Though Satan would wish to topple that spiritual temple of ours, we may stand secure against his invasion. Though he is an enemy more powerful than the invading Roman army that laid the Temple of Jerusalem to ruin in 70 A.D., we may resist his attacks with the aid of divine grace. Strengthened by the spiritual nourishment of Word and Sacrament, we may persevere in running the race of faith and finishing the marathon that matters.

As per her request, we celebrated a Mass in her new room in the Care Center with five of her family and friends, and she received a small particle of the Sacred Host. This was on the Wednesday afternoon before Thanksgiving Day. Two days later, on Friday afternoon, she reached the finish line of her marathon and received the crown of eternal life.

Go for the Gold

Paul speaks of the race and the crown in writing to Timothy:

> "I have fought the good fight, I have finished the race, I have kept the faith. From now on there is laid up for me the crown of righteousness, which the Lord, the righteous judge, will award to me on that Day, and not only to me but to all who have loved his appearing." (2 Tim 4:7-8)

The letter to the Hebrews encourages us all to persevere in the race of faith:

> "Therefore, since we are surrounded by so great a cloud of witnesses, let us also lay aside every weight, and sin which clings so closely, and let us run with perseverance the race that is set before us, looking to Jesus the pioneer and perfecter of our faith, who for the joy that was set before him endured the cross, despising the shame, and is seated at the right hand of the throne of God." (Heb 12:1-2)

One of the most exhilarating aspects of participating in races held in the larger cities is the crowd applauding, cheering, and urging the runners on. I experienced this uplifting crowd support during marathons in Fargo, Duluth, Minneapolis, Winnipeg, Chicago, and Boston. Applying this to our spiritual race, we have a cloud of witnesses in the saints who cheer us on from their place in heaven through their intercession on our behalf.

We never run our race alone. On the Fourteenth of September 2021, as I lay in Sanford Hospital after the initial surgical repair of my injuries, I was already surrounded by a cloud of earthly witnesses, the living friends and community members praying for me. News had spread so rapidly that within a few days I received cards and prayer support from over two hundred members of parishes I had served previously, my current parishes and the Christian churches of the towns I serve. Their prayer support lifted my spirits and gave me courage to persevere in the marathon of recovery, the long race just begun.

Throughout the following year of my recovery marathon, I felt a solidarity with persons suffering maladies of many kinds. Bedridden for a brief time, though never paralyzed, I felt deeper compassion for those who cannot rise from bed or perform simple tasks by themselves. Wheelchair bound for a time and needing two aides to lift me up and transport me from bed to bathroom, I shared the lot of many nursing home residents and disabled persons of any age. While learning to ambulate with walker and cane, I found solidarity with a great number of aging senior citizens. As of this writing, my weaker left knee will not sustain the impact of running, though I continue to walk with greater facility.

Most of us may never complete a marathon of the physical running kind. Yet we are all engaged in the race Paul describes -- the race for the prize of eternal life with the saints of heaven. Olympic gold medalists are a rare and special kind of athlete. Yet Paul urges each of us to "run so as to win." (I Cor 9:24)

The merited crown of eternal happiness awaits those who persevere in following the Way, heeding the voice of Truth spoken by the Word made flesh, and living the Life exemplified by our Savior. In so doing, we will inhabit the dwelling Christ has gone to prepare for us. (Cf. Jn 14:1-6)

I want to use the time I have left in this world to prepare well for the next life, doing my best to please the Lord and serve his people each day. I pray you will do the same. Have the finish line fixed in mind as you plod forward, step by daily step.

Go for the Gold in the Marathon that Matters.

30 Triumph of the Cross

Let me conclude where we began, noting the day on which my accident occurred. September 14 is our annual observance of the Feast of the Exaltation (Triumph) of the Holy Cross. That feast recalls the great events of the finding of the True Cross by Saint Helena, and the September 14 dedication of churches built by her son, Emperor Constantine, on the sites of the Holy Sepulcher and Mount Calvary in 335 AD.

Credible legend has it that Saint Helena discovered three crosses upon excavation under the pagan temple of Venus which the Romans had built over the site of Golgotha.

"When the three crosses were excavated, the bishop of Jerusalem, Macarius, proposed a sure means of confirming which was the True one. They were taken to the bedside of a distinguished lady who was dangerously ill. As the bishop prayed for a revelation, the touch of the True Cross immediately cured her. Helena at once ordered the construction of a magnificent basilica over the spot where the cross had been found."[1]

"According to the message of Eusebius of Caesarea before the battle of the Mulvian Bridge (October 28, 312 CE) Constantine the Great had a vision that allowed him to win. Around noon he was to see a luminous cross in the sky, and under it the inscription in Greek, 'In this, conquer.' Better known in Latin translation *'In hoc signo vinces'* – 'In this sign thou shalt conquer.' The next night in a dream, Christ commanded him to use the sign of the cross against his enemies. Eusebius then describes a *labarum* (legionary banner) with the sign *Chi Rho* (first two Greek letters of the word for Christ). Constantine was the first emperor to convert to Christianity. He ended the policy of persecuting Christians and in 313 issued the Edict of Milan, proclaiming the freedom to profess this religion."[2]

Whether the True Cross on which Christ hung on Calvary had ever been discovered or not, the reality of Christ's triumphant death and resurrection remains the same. By his loving act of sacrifice, Christ conquered Satan once and for all, winning the victory of eternal salvation for all humankind. We who bear the cross of discipleship, who "deny ourselves, take up the cross and follow him," may anticipate a share in that victory. (Cf. Mk 8:34, Lk 9:23)

In this sign, then, we too shall conquer. Taking up our personal cross entails self-denial of many kinds. Surrendering ourselves to the will of God, we freely renounce those sinful thoughts, words and deeds that would distance ourselves from our loving Father. Embracing the call of discipleship, we take up a sacrificial lifestyle of Christlike love for God and neighbor. We may also be nailed to crosses of suffering in body and spirit. We may unite ourselves with Christ in his agonized prayer in the Garden of Gethsemane, "Father, if you are willing, take this cup away from me; still, not my will but yours be done." (Lk 22:42)

We would never wish such agony upon ourselves nor wish to impose such burdens on others. It was not God's original intent, nor is it God's final will, for humanity to suffer so.

"As long as he remained in the divine intimacy, man would not have to suffer or die." (CCC 376, citing Gen 2:17 and 3:16,19)

"Now the Father's will is 'to raise up men to share in his own divine life.'" (CCC 541, citing *Lumen Gentium* 2)

Sadly, much of the worst suffering we bear comes from sinful humanity itself, from the evil we do to one another or the harm we inflict upon ourselves.

When faced with crosses we neither asked for nor anticipated, Christlike disciples will accept them as part of our walk to Calvary with the Redeemer. We may experience our personal *Via Dolorosa,* our Way of the Cross, as people familiar with that popular Lenten devotion may wish to call their suffering. We may fall several times along the way. We may meet our personal mother Mary and other faithful followers to weep with us and to console us. We may meet a Veronica to wipe the bloody sweat from our face. We may encounter a Simon to share our burden and lighten our load. Still, we will find ourselves there with Jesus on Golgotha, sharing in the pains of his crucifixion.

On one hand, I find myself identifying with Christ in the various forms of suffering I have encountered on this life's journey. On the other hand, I can more readily identify with the repentant thief who hung beside him, well deserving of my suffering as punishment for my sins.

"And indeed, we have been condemned justly, for the sentence we received corresponds to our crimes, but this man has done nothing wrong. Jesus, remember me when you come into your kingdom." (Lk 23:41-42)

Gladly, thankfully, my accident of September 14 was not to end in death that day. God spared me, I believe, so that I could willingly bear whatever cross of suffering was yet to come and take up the burden of following Christ more faithfully. The inevitable will come on the day and the hour known to God alone. I envisioned my mother Mildred remarking during that nanosecond of the Celestial Conference, "He will be with us soon enough."

On that day, may I hear Jesus' word to the repentant thief, "Amen I say to you, today you will be with me in Paradise." (Lk 23:43) On that day, may I join the cloud of witnesses who cheered me on, and share in the Triumph of the Holy Cross.

---

[1]A.R. Birley, "Helena, Discoverer of the True Cross," Brown University, https://www.brown.edu/Research/Breaking_Ground/bios/St.%20Helena_Flavia%20Julia%20Helena%20Augusta.pdf

[2]https://imperiumromanum.pl, June 29, 2021

31 Summary Sentiments

On September 14, 2021, the Feast of the Exaltation of the Holy Cross, I came within three feet of death while on the road to Cooperstown. It would be the greatest physical cross I had borne up to that time. While mercifully sparing me from death, God gave me this opportunity to embrace my cross and identify more closely with the suffering of Jesus Christ. The Cross he bore upon his shoulders, falling under its weight on the way to Calvary, would become the instrument of our salvation. My cross would become the instrument of a personal awakening to the love of God calling me to renewed discipleship and faithful service.

While in the hospital and while engaged in the slow, steady, ongoing process of rehabilitation and recovery, I was given the opportunity to identify with the many who suffer more permanent forms of disability of the same kind. I gained greater respect for those who bear their crosses with grace and dignity. I admire those who patiently accept their limitations without complaint, and who make their best effort to live fully to the extent of their ability despite, or even because of, these challenges.

In quest of renewed balance of the disciplines of body, mind, and spirit, I have intensified my dedication to prayer, to study of the Word of God, and service to God's People on into my years of retirement. The full nature of that service has yet to be determined, but I will discern that as the years unfold. The plan I have already submitted to God in prayer seems to be unfolding as I had hoped. Letting go of any feelings of guilt for failing to become a missionary to the poorest countries of the world, I will choose ordinary opportunities to serve as they arise, wherever I live. We are needed here at home too, to work among the spiritually poor of our own land.

My days of running, of marathons and Ironman Triathlons and long-distance cycling are done. I have surrendered my plans to through-hike the entire Appalachian Trail, although God willing, I may trek pieces of it as able. I surrender the thrill of such cardiovascular accomplishments and pass the Olympian's torch on to the next generation of dedicated fitness afficionados. But I will never surrender the determination to do whatever I am capable of with the body God gave me.

Finally, recognizing my life in "the womb of the earth" is now in its third trimester, as it were, I begin to focus more fully on preparation for my birth into the life of eternity. Considering this earth as the womb in which we are nurtured while we develop into full maturity and readiness for delivery into the wondrous world of the saints, I want to let go of the attachments hindering me from those final stages of development.

> "If then you were raised with Christ, seek what is above, where Christ is seated at the right hand of God. Think of what is above, not of what is on earth. For you have died, and your life is hidden with Christ in God. When Christ your life appears, you too will appear with him in glory." (Col 3:1-4)

Thinking of what is above, I bear the scars of my injuries in union with Christ wounded for us. Miraculously spared from death of the body on this occasion, I renew my quest of life with Christ in the Resurrection. May we all renew this same quest with greater resolve, without needing to be three feet from death to do so.

My soul, at that instant of bodily collision, screamed, "Lord, is this how I am going to die? I'm not ready yet!" What might you and I yet need to do, to change, to be ready if we should be called home today or tomorrow?

The reflections contained in this work are written not merely for my benefit. What I have shared is meant to issue an invitation and a challenge, for every reader, every disciple, to heed the call of Christ to "deny yourself, *take up your cross*, and follow me." (Cf. Mt 16:24-25)

Deny yourself: What ought I surrender, give up, stop thinking or saying or doing, to purge myself of those things which displease God, those areas of sin to which I have still been clinging?

Take up your cross. What ought I begin doing, or continue to do more faithfully, to fulfill my calling? This may include any hardships and suffering with which we may more closely identify with the redeeming sacrifice of Christ on Calvary. In so doing, we will better please God and grow more deeply in union with Jesus who said, "Take my yoke upon you and learn from me, for I am meek and humble of heart; and you will find rest for yourselves. For my yoke is easy, and my burden light." (Mt 11:28-29)

For some, perhaps for many, taking up the yoke of Jesus may mean beginning or resuming a life of prayer, attending Sunday worship in obedience to the command to "remember keep holy the Sabbath day," and taking more seriously the great commandment to "love the Lord your God, with all your heart and soul and mind," and to "love your neighbor as yourself." (Cf. Mt 21:34-40)

Follow me. Jesus Christ came in human flesh, to show us by word and example how to live the perfect life. While we cannot expect perfection here on earth, we can, with the aid of divine grace, do our best to emulate him in our thoughts, our words, and our lifestyle.

"I am the way and the truth and the life. No one comes to the Father except through me." (Jn 14:6) Deeper union with Christ will ensure our journey is headed in the right direction, to the dwelling place he has gone ahead to prepare for us.

32 Postscript

August 20, 2023

I set out from Cooperstown Sunday afternoon after Masses, arriving in Olympia, Washington, by suppertime Monday. I drove fifteen hundred miles to the Pacific Northwest in response to the invitation of a newfound hiking companion: Dale Baird, of whom I wrote in Chapter 29. He had come to Cooperstown to assist his sister, Gretchen, during her final stages of terminal cancer, staying with her through her death and funeral. We had conversed and compared cardiovascular activity interests, hence the invitation.

On Tuesday morning, Dale and I set out on a hiking loop of one of the mountain trails in Olympic National Park. Wednesday found us hiking a loop of the Mount Rainier National Park, negotiating some 3500 feet of ascent at the base of the big mountain on a foggy morning.

On both hikes, I managed the ascent portion quite handily, thanks to my trekking poles and renewed endurance. The descent was another matter altogether. My left knee was not yet ready to negotiate the steep rugged trail's roots and rocks. Gingerly working my way downward, I would plant the poles, let the left foot down first and bring the right foot alongside, then repeat the process. It felt as if I were back in physical therapy at the Cooperstown Medical Center, with Sarah urging me to give it a go. Dale would descend a couple hundred yards ahead of me and then patiently wait for me to catch up before moving on down the trail. Young and old alike were cruising by as I stepped aside, allowing them passage. I would smile and comment, "Appreciate your two good knees while you have them!"

Returning home from this effort, discouraged by the relatively poor performance of my left knee, I resolved to resume the self-prescribed therapy I had been neglecting. For a year or more I had contented myself with my ability to walk level stretches at a decent pace, without doing much to strengthen the quad tendon.

Our church sacristy is connected to the parish office by a hallway with a flight of eight stair steps. This would become my handy therapy tool. Eschewing the handrails, I would tell myself, "Okay, left knee, do your thing! Slowly lower yourself to the next step, no rails, don't baby yourself!" Doing this several times a day, I have already noted remarkable progress in knee strength. "You get what you pay for," I remarked to that inner self.

My physical healing is satisfyingly complete, even though I still experience a weakness in the quadriceps tendon. The challenges it presents in my effort to descend a flight of stairs, or a mountain slope, serve as a visible reminder of the pesky habits of sin, the lingering weakness of our spiritual knees, that cause the faltering steps in our heavenward journey.

October 26, 2023

It was a rainy Thursday afternoon. The local forecast called for snow overnight, the first snowfall of late autumn. I set out for Grand Forks, an eighty-five-mile drive, intent on completing some business, and stayed overnight so as not to drive back in the dark in snowy conditions.

Upon waking early Friday morning, I discovered Grand Forks already had six inches of snow. I swept the white blanket away from my vehicle with the brush I had brought along. The ground was snow-covered, but the major roadways had been plowed and were passable. I merged onto Interstate 29 from Highway 2 at 7:30 am, just before sunrise. The road surface was slick, so I worked my way south at a cautious 45 miles per hour, staying in the right lane. Sixth sense and peripheral vision prompted me to glance to my right at the next interchange, where I spied a black vehicle merging from the on-ramp at the same rate of speed. Moving into the left lane to allow him entry, my black Chevy Trax went into a skid on that icier less-used left lane. Now my reflexes and driving skills were tested to the limit as I negotiated a quadruple set of left-right-left turns of the steering wheel, no foot on the brakes and no accelerator.

"I hope this guy remembers to yield next time," I thought, after recovering from what could have easily been a rollover in the ditch to the left, or a collision with the car beside me. The driver of that merging vehicle should have slowed down to move in behind me. Ordinarily, in daylight and on a decent road surface, I would have gladly moved into the left lane earlier, but I did not see this fellow until he had nearly pushed me over in his effort to merge.

After this incident, as my blood pressure calmed and my heart returned to normal rhythm, I realized these things can happen so easily. That day, I could have wound up in the Grand Forks Hospital or the morgue, thanks to this latest Close Encounter of the Automobile Kind. I have been extremely fortunate so far, but one day I am finally going to run out of cat-lives. Was this the ninth of ten?

Be vigilant, be ready, "stay awake, for you know neither the day nor the hour." (Mt 25:13)

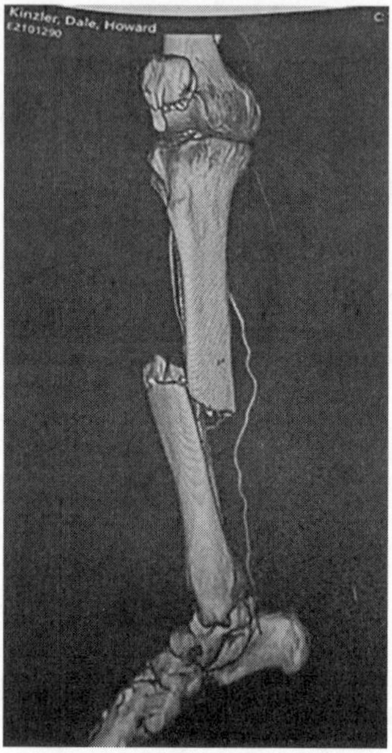

Fractured right leg
9/14/2021

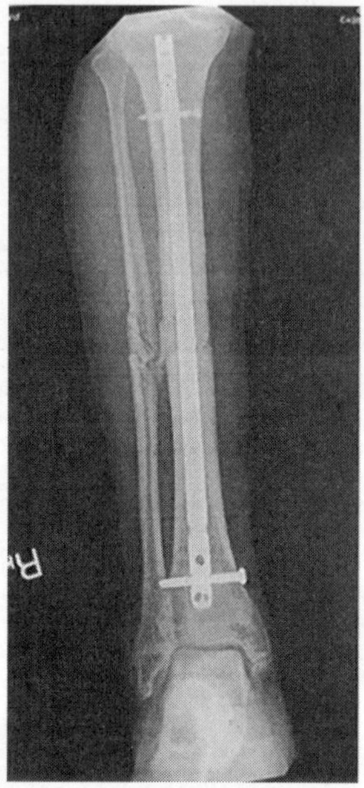

Repair x-ray
10/28/21

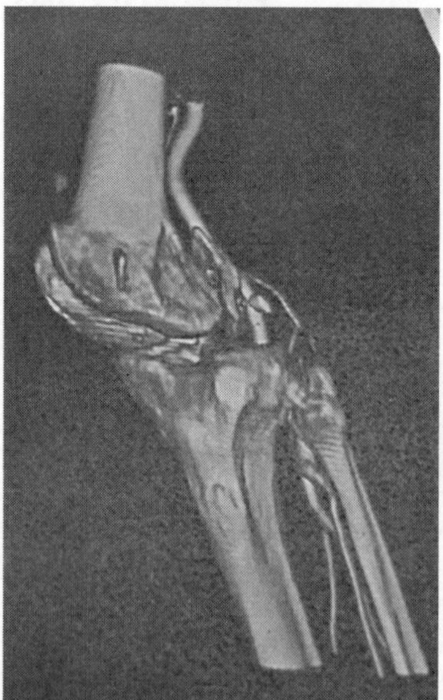

Ruptured left knee
9/14/21

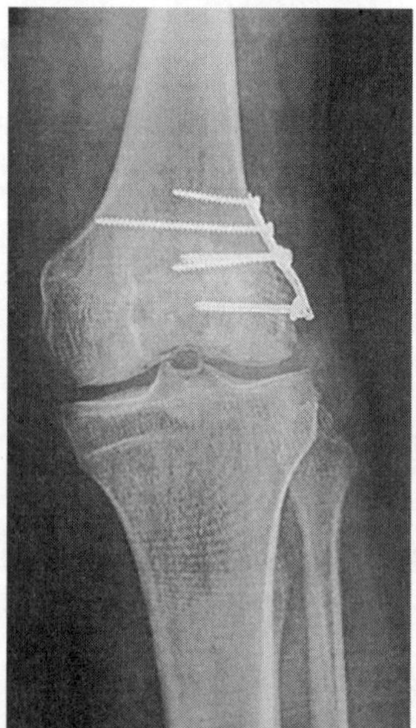

Repair surgery
9/22/21

X-ray photos courtesy of Sanford Orthopedics Hospital, Fargo, ND

Cover Photo Credits:

Alero on flatbed, Courtesy of Jeffrey Kenninger, Cooperstown, ND

Fire and Rescue workers, Courtesy of Meghan Ressler, Cooperstown, ND

Acknowledgments